STARVED BIBLE STUDY

STARVED

BIBLE STUDY

A
SIX-WEEK
GUIDED
JOURNEY

A Tyndale nonfiction imprint

Visit Tyndale online at tyndale.com.

Visit Tyndale Momentum online at tyndalemomentum.com.

Visit the author at amyseiffert.com.

Tyndale, Tyndale's quill logo, *Tyndale Momentum*, and the Tyndale Momentum logo are registered trademarks of Tyndale House Ministries. Tyndale Momentum is a nonfiction imprint of Tyndale House Publishers, Carol Stream, Illinois.

Starved Bible Study: A Six-Week Guided Journey

Designed by Jennifer Phelps

For information about special discounts for bulk purchases, please contact Tyndale House Publishers at csresponse@tyndale.com, or call 1-855-277-9400.

ISBN 978-1-4964-6033-2

Printed in China

29	28	27	26	25	24	23
7	6	5	4	3	2	1

CONTENTS

A NOTE TO THE LEADER

LISTEN UP, MY DEAR FRIEND.

You can do this.

You don't have to have a theology degree, or the perfect marriage, or children who behave like cherubs, or any part of your life totally figured out to do this. Trust me when I tell you that I have none of those things.

You don't have to be old and wise.

You don't have to be hip and swag.

You can be you, and you can lead this thing.

Why?

Because the Holy Spirit lives in you.

And because the disciples were uneducated fishermen.

Those two reasons alone should breathe life into any insecurities about leading this Bible study. You've been called by God and equipped with His Spirit. That, my friend, is all you need.

This group of fellow travelers is starved to see other humans trusting God and taking steps of faith. And I promise, you will be nourished by leading. Stay humble, trust Jesus, and watch as He uses your leading to nourish others, just as He will nourish you.

Over the years, I have mentored dozens of women in college (and older) on how to lead a Bible study or a spiritual group discussion. I'd love to share a few of my best tips with you as you begin.

SNACKS

Ask someone each week to bring some kind of snack. Store bought or home-made, sweet or salty, it doesn't matter. Something happens when food is involved—something good. It becomes a fellowship and a way to break the ice of coming together. Yes, the snacks are essential.

PRAYER

After about fifteen minutes of informal hang-out with your chips and guacamole, gather everyone up and start by praying for your time. Besides being a great cue to let everyone know you're about to begin, it's also a chance to invite the Lord to work in and through your time together.

THE "THREE THEN ME" RULE

Let the group know you are going to follow the "Three Then Me" rule for discussion. This is where group members let three other people share before they share again. It helps us make space for all kinds of people in the group. This way, no one dominates. Feel free to state this each week to remind the talkers in the group of the format you want to follow.

QUESTIONS

This is a six-week study. Each week you meet, you'll cover one topic. You could walk through each day and ask a variety of questions to get the group talking. All you really have to do is ask good questions here. You can pull some from the study or ask the Lord to lead you in coming up with some of your own. As you personally answer, lead with humility and vulnerability. You don't need to fix or solve anyone. Listening and empathy are two of the biggest parts of leadership.

A few questions to get you started:

- What spoke to you or what did you underline on this day?
- What did you discover about God's character on this day?
- What did you discover about yourself on this day?
- Did you do the spiritual practices at the end? How were those for your relationship with God?

DON'T BE AFRAID OF SILENCE

Don't feel the need to fill the space. Silence is often a space to let the internal processors find their words. While you don't want to linger so long that it becomes distracting, don't be afraid to sit in the silence for a while to let those have it who need it.

PRAYER . . . AGAIN

Close your group in prayer. Here are a few prayer tips to consider for this:

- Pray to God. Don't pray with mini-sermons for someone else. (For example, don't pray, "Dear God, please help Amy to see how wrong she is, and that she needs to call her sister right away, and she needs to repent, and she needs to. . . .")
- Pray about real heart change for yourself and your group. Try to stick to praying about the content of the week. That will keep the focus of your prayers on the material you discussed.
- Let people know they don't have to pray at all. This isn't a requirement; it's an invitation. So, if someone doesn't feel comfortable, they can pray quietly or listen as someone else prays.

Underlined heavily in my Bible is this verse from a beloved psalm: "The LORD will accomplish what concerns me; your faithfulness, LORD, is everlasting; do not abandon the works of Your hands" (Psalm 138:8, NASB).

You are the work of His hands, and He will not abandon you. He will accomplish what concerns you! And this is what is in front of you.

I am cheering you on, and I believe that God will equip you to do this good work.

Have fun, and be blessed!

Amy

INTRODUCTION

Listen to me, listen well: Eat only the best, fill yourself with only the finest.
ISAIAH 55:2, MSG

DEAR FRIEND,

I'm willing to bet the farm you feel it.

Because if you're anything like me—*human*—then you know what I'm talking about.

The nagging spiritual hunger pangs in your heart.

The exhaustion, anxiety, and dissatisfaction that fill your plate without filling your stomach.

The attempt to nourish yourself with anything that you think will satiate.

The starvation deep in your soul.

The menu we keep choosing from to satisfy our hunger promises substance, but in reality, it eventually falls flat. Much like the way a soufflé behaves—coming out hot, pretty, and puffed up before quickly lying back down in the pan as if it's nap time—what we're consuming appears delightful on the outside but is nothing more than fluff once we get down to it. So, we keep trying new recipes, keep changing ingredients, keep attempting new meals that we think will finally cure our hunger. Podcasts, social media, perfectionism, the opinions of others, cute shoes, overworking—these all hold some morsel of nutrition, sure, but none that will last.

Friend, we may be eating, but still, we are starving.

I know this feeling deep in my bones.

I know it after a few minutes turns into hours on my phone, and I feel worse, not better.

I know it after I work harder than I ever have to achieve, only to be left wondering what's next at the end of the day.

1

I know it when I believe there is joy to be found in consumerism, but it ultimately consumes me instead.

I know it when anxiety rises as I try to shoulder the weight of the world, only to realize my human shoulders can't take it.

I know what starvation is because I've felt it too.

And I wrote the book *Starved* because I was tired of feeling it. I kept running to the same things for satisfaction, but they only got me halfway there. And some of them? They actually plucked me up and placed me farther away from nourishment than where I began. They sold me the lie that they would bring me to a banquet table, but they left me outside looking for scraps. So, I simply decided: No more!

No more hunger.

No more searching.

No more trying to feed myself with the things that won't satisfy.

No more starvation.

It's time to feast on the things that will nourish. It's time to feast on the things of God.

I wrote this study as a companion to *Starved*. It's designed to help you go deeper in your study of Scripture. It's here to help you sweep out your spiritual pantry and replace those old ingredients with new spiritual practices and principles that will nourish you in real, lasting ways. Because we're only diving in for six weeks together here, this study will cover six of the topics touched on in *Starved*. I wish we had more time to go over each and every single one in detail together, but for now, we'll just agree to start here.

Six topics, six truths, six practices, six principles, six weeks of walking out of starvation and into satisfaction.

I do hope you'll read *Starved* as a companion to this study, either with a small group or on your own. Because in doing so, I believe you will find yourself eating good food and living abundantly. I believe you'll begin to truly live because your food is truly sustaining.

I believe it will help you finally begin to feast.

This study you're holding was created with you in mind. You want God. You want to feel whole. You want to engage in practices that bring satisfaction, nourishment, and peace. You want to leave behind sluggish spirituality, and you want to "fill yourself with only the finest," according to what is good to God. You want someone to tell you that God is good and can truly, deeply satisfy you.

But fair warning, friend. The thing about enjoying nourishment in Christ is that a few changes have to be made to get there. We need to examine what we believe. We need to exchange the lies for the truth. We need to gently engage in practices that spur our body, soul, and mind to actually change.

This study invites you to join me in practicing, not perfecting. I want to welcome you to the table, invite you to sit down with me and give thanks, and begin the good and holy work of seeking spiritual nourishment from Jesus.

Jesus said that if anyone was thirsty or hungry, they could come to Him. That invitation is for us. We can come together; we don't have to go alone. He loves when we grab one another and run together to His beautiful banquet table. So friend, let's agree to walk forward to take our seat at His table—the one paid for with His love. Let's agree to leave behind what's starving us in order to fill our hearts with what will satisfy: Jesus.

> Come, buy your drinks, buy wine and milk.
>> Buy without money—everything's free!
> Why do you spend your money on junk food,
>> your hard-earned cash on cotton candy?
> Listen to me, listen well: Eat only the best,
>> fill yourself with only the finest.
> Pay attention, come close now,
>> listen carefully to my life-giving, life-nourishing words.
> I'm making a lasting covenant commitment with you,
>> the same that I made with David: sure, solid, enduring love.

ISAIAH 55:1-4, MSG

Coming, listening, and eating what is good with you, *Amy*

STARVED FOR CONNECTION

Questions for Discussion

THE PROBLEM
What is starving us in our quest for connection?

THE PROMISE
What Scriptures have been feeding your soul lately?

THE PRACTICE
What spiritual practices can satiate you when your soul is feeling starved for connection?

PERSONAL REFLECTION
Choose a question and take a moment to journal your response.

- Have you ever paid attention to how much time you spend on your phone? If so, what did you discover?
- What do you believe about your phone? Write as many positive and negative statements as you can.
- What is true about God's character? How does this help you when it comes to true connection?

STARVED FOR CONNECTION

To get the most out of this week's study, read chapter 1 of *Starved*.

CHOCOLATE FOR BROCCOLI

No eggs.

Not again. Why do I always run out of eggs when I need to bake something? And why am I mid-recipe with flour, baking powder, and vanilla all positioned in the bowl, ready to be whipped up into something fabulous when I realize this? Why didn't I look before I started this cooking journey?

Please tell me this happens to you, too.

And then of course, the Internet search begins: "What are egg substitutions?"

Applesauce? I'm out.

Flax? Out.

Chia? Nope.

Arrowroot? No dice.

Banana? YES.

SWEET! Now we're cooking . . . or baking.

The substitution struggle is real. That cookie recipe wasn't going to work if I didn't have some kind of binding and rising agent. It was going to be flat, underwhelming, and weird. I couldn't just leave it out. I needed to replace the missing ingredient with something just as good—brownie points if it was even better.

The same is true when ingredients are missing from our spiritual diets, friend. When what we're using isn't working or we don't have what we need in our pantry, we've got to find a replacement.

Something good. Something better. Something that will satisfy.

In this first week of our study together, we are taking a good look at the small rectangular devices in our pockets. And yes, I will be the first to admit I have a phone addiction. I'd venture to say you might, as well.

The numbers don't lie, friends.

- 71 percent check their phone right after waking up.
- 74 percent feel nervous if they leave their phone at home.
- 35 percent look at (or use) their phone while driving.
- 47 percent are addicted to their phone, by their own admission.
- 53 percent say they have never gone more than a full day without their phone.
- 48 percent feel panicky when their battery is low.
- 62 percent have their phone by their bed at night.
- 45 percent consider their phone their most valuable possession.[1]

Now let's be honest. At first glance, this feels like an unfair trade. Trading out our phones for silence feels like trading chocolate for broccoli.

And well, it kind of is, but hear me out. Broccoli, over time, is nourishing for a million reasons. Drizzled with olive oil, sprinkled with kosher salt, and roasted at 425 degrees for 30 minutes? Then, it's not just nourishing, it's good. But chocolate over time? Sadly, it's not so nourishing. Sure, it gives a quick sugar high, a fix of energy, and a delicious taste. But is it chock-full of vitamins? Can it help detoxify your body? Is it an anti-inflammatory? Nope. So even though it's good, over time, it won't satisfy. If we ate chocolate all day every day? Well, we would starve.

The same is true when it comes to our souls. What we consume, we become. If we take in photo after photo of beautiful people in beautiful houses with picture-perfect lives? We may try to become picture perfect, a defeating and unrealistic endeavor we'll never achieve. If we consume copious amounts of articles or podcasts on fashion or scientific developments or the latest celebrity scandals? We'll think about these things in copious amounts. We will be shaped and formed by the information we take in, for better or for worse. If we live and die by the text messages, calendars, notifications, and apps on our phones? We'll become enslaved to the devices in our hands.

That's why we've got to make a trade. Chocolate for broccoli, our phones for our sanity.

I know this one is hard. Because phones are tricky. A phone in and of itself is not bad. We can communicate, we can work, we can create, we can encourage, we can laugh, we can play, we can connect, we can share—all with our phones. But at the same time, our phones can steal our agency from us by telling us what to think about, causing anxiety with every news source and notification we get. They can push us to comparison, jealousy, fear, envy, worry, insecurity, and more. If we're not careful, that little device meant for connection can disconnect us from everything and everyone that might actually satisfy us. Yes, we were created for connection, and our phones—the very advertisement of connection—are disconnecting our souls.

They're starving us from it.

So how do we change our steady diet? How do we overcome what might be a downright addiction to our phones? By creating space to acknowledge what's starving us and turning our hearts to the One who can nourish us.

That's what I hope we'll begin to do together over the course of this week's study. As we examine the way our habits with our phones may be impacting our spiritual diets, my prayer is that our hearts will be open to confess what we've been trying to find in that device. That we'll be spurred on to make a trade, giving up what's starving us in favor of what will truly, deeply nourish us.

PUT DOWN THE PHONE, FRIEND

When it comes to your phone (or any screen time), what do you believe it will do for you?

In what ways does your phone fail to deliver what you're looking for?

For me, I believe my phone will help me get work done. I believe my phone will validate me when I see the likes on my social media page. I believe my phone will show me great new recipes and amazing new fashion. I believe it will help me communicate with all my friends.

When I look at that list, I realize I'm asking a lot of my phone.

Does it deliver? In the short run, yes. I do get a lot of work done on my phone. I do find some validation on social media. I am able to connect with my people, both those close by and those across long distances.

But maybe, if I dig just a layer deeper, there's more to it than that. Because if that was all it was, would I really be starving for more each night I plugged that device in to charge?

I wonder if this question rings as true for you as it does for me: *Do I believe my phone will take care of me?*

It's a question worth asking. Why is that little device so often our everything? What do I believe about God or myself when it comes to my phone? What am I avoiding in myself with each swipe to unlock that precious device? Do I believe my phone will take care of me?

My answer to this question is convicting. I have found it helpful to do two things when it comes to dealing with this in my own life: confess my struggle to believe that God will take care of me, and ask God to help me believe He will take care of me. Along with that simple prayer, I have learned to substitute my phone with true connection—connection to God, to myself, and to those in front of me.

The practice of silence has become one of the ways I continue to recover true connection. It gives me the space to confess my struggles—to lay out on the table what is starving me from the goodness of connection with God. It allows me to sit in the belief that God will take care of me. That He is big enough to take care of me no matter what. That He wants to connect with me.

If I am quiet.

If I am lonely.

If I am afraid.

If I am bitter.

If I am weak.

If I stop checking things off the list.

If I take time off.

If I stop pushing and proving, answering emails, and folding clothes.

If I stop being so manicured.

If I am anxious.

If I am unproductive.

In the silence, I confess that I haven't always believed this is true of God. That's what's at the root of my phone addiction. That's what's causing my starvation.

And maybe, friend, the same is true for you.

So, the question we want to answer this week is this: *Will God take care of me?*

We need to start by simply discovering more about who God is. Who does God say He is? Who does He declare Himself to be?

One of the foundational moments where God tells us who He is comes from the second book of the Bible. Very early on, God wants to set the record straight. So, before God's people received His commands or rules for living well, He told them who He was.

Before they received the Ten Commandments, they received the character of God. And because of who He is, we can trust that God's way—about to be etched in stone—is good for us. Mind you, this was the second time God gave the Ten Commandments—what grace after their sin (see Exodus 32:1-20).

> He passed in front of Moses, proclaiming, "The LORD, the LORD, the compassionate and gracious God, slow to anger, abounding in love and faithfulness." EXODUS 34:6, NIV

This beautiful description of God is what the women and men of old come back to over and over throughout the Bible. They call upon God's character and come back to this declaration from God about Himself. Why? Well, because that's where they find real nourishment. It's where they can begin to connect with who God really is.

Read Exodus 34:1-14. Where was Moses at this time?

According to verse 5, what was the Lord about to proclaim?

God is proclaiming His name. Make a list of the five attributes God uses to describe Himself in Exodus 34:6.

1.

2.

3.

4.

5.

Today we will look at the first attribute of God listed in this passage. **Circle that first word.**

Here's a confession for you: I strongly dislike math and equations. I'm more of a word girl. That's why I've found this one equation to be extremely helpful—because it has words, not numbers.

Empathy + Action = Compassion

Empathy is the idea of putting ourselves in another's shoes and feeling what they're feeling. And, as the equation demonstrates, it's when we put that empathy into action that compassion is born. Compassion starts walking in those shoes and does something to address the issue.

I love how *Greater Good* magazine—where they turn scientific research into stories, tips, and tools for a more compassionate society—puts it:

> While cynics may dismiss compassion as touchy-feely or irrational, scientists have started to map the biological basis of compassion. . . . This research has shown that when we feel compassion, our heart rate slows down, we secrete the "bonding hormone" oxytocin, and regions of the brain linked to empathy, caregiving, and feelings of pleasure light up, which often results in our wanting to approach and care for other people.[1]

This is the God we serve! A God who has feelings of empathy, caregiving, and pleasure that light up inside of Him for us. A God who longs to bond with us. A God who wants to nurture and care for us as His children. A God who leads with compassion.

If God is compassionate, that means Jesus is too. Let's check the math on this.

Read these verses below. As you do, underline the word compassion. Then circle the way you see Jesus showing compassion in action.

> Moved with compassion, Jesus touched their eyes; and immediately they regained their sight and followed Him.
> MATTHEW 20:34, NASB

> When the Lord saw her, He felt compassion for her and said to her, "Do not go on weeping."
> LUKE 7:13, NASB

> Jesus called His disciples to Him and said, "I feel compassion for the people, because they have remained with Me now for three days and have nothing to eat; and I do not want to send them away hungry, for they might faint on the way."
> MATTHEW 15:32, NASB

> When He came ashore, He saw a large crowd, and felt compassion for them and healed their sick.
> MATTHEW 14:14, NASB

> When Jesus went ashore, He saw a large crowd, and He felt compassion for them because they were like sheep without a shepherd; and He began to teach them many things.
> MARK 6:34, NASB

The ultimate act of compassion was the Cross. It was the entire purpose of Jesus' coming. *Compassion carried Christ to the Cross.* He saw our sinful and separated situation from our Creator; He saw us starving. So He literally put on human skin (empathy) to live among us and endure the Cross (action). Why? So that God's wrath was justly poured out upon our sin but unjustly and graciously poured out on His innocent Son.

Our God is a compassionate God.

We can trust Him to care for us. To provide for us. To reassure us that we can stand securely. We can trust that God sees us and is moving toward us. That He will not leave us alone but will be with us in our silence.

We can trust that when we feel rejected, He will not reject us. That when we feel abandoned, He will not abandon us. That when we feel unloved, He will love us. That when we put our phone down, He will pick us up.

> We can trust that God sees us and is moving toward us. That He will not leave us alone but will be with us in our silence.

Today, how do you need our compassionate God to take care of you? Is it regarding your identity, your reputation, your finances, your anxiety, or your fears? List the areas you struggle to believe God is compassionately caring for you.

Confess these struggles to the Lord and ask for His compassion to be evident in your life.

THE PRACTICE OF CONNECTION

One of the best things we can do to find nourishment is to connect with the compassionate God we serve. To help us do this, we will end each day this week with a few minutes of silence. We will start with five minutes today, adding one minute each day to end with nine full minutes of silence by the end of the week.

In order to prepare for this time of silence, put your phone away. If it helps to set an alarm for five minutes, go ahead and get that ready. Turn off any music, television, noise, or screens. Maybe go outside if you can. If you have not practiced being quiet very often, the first few minutes may be very difficult as your mind wanders. You may feel anxious. You may think of every kind of thing you need to be doing. You may be uncomfortable. If that happens to you, don't worry! You are not a failure in this. This is quite normal!

Just breathe. Take in your surroundings. Using your senses, notice nature—the sights of trees or flowers, sounds of birds or animals, feelings of grass or snow. Trust God that your to-do list will still be there. Trust God that He will take care of you if you rest. Trust God to run your world. Trust God to be God. Trust God to care for you. Trust God to connect with you in these moments of silence and beyond.

If it helps, here is a breath prayer you can use during your five minutes. Inhale for four counts (one word for each count). Exhale for five counts (one word for each count).

Inhale: God, you are compassionate.
Exhale: I am in Your care.

> **BONUS:** Record how this first moment of silence was for you. What was your practice of silence like? As Aundi Kolber says, pay "compassionate attention" to yourself.[2] Your feelings are neither good nor bad; they are messengers telling you something. Be kind to them and to yourself, as God is compassionate to you.

THE THRONE OF WHAT?

Yesterday we looked at God's compassionate heart for us. He is a God who sees us, slips on our shoes, and strides toward us with empathy and action. Who went to the greatest lengths possible to take care of us by repairing our souls with His blood. Who wants to find us in our starvation and nourish us with His presence.

Today, let's look at the second attribute God declares about Himself from His monumental moment with Moses on the mountain. Because the more we understand God's character, the more we'll find ourselves eager to disconnect from what isn't feeding us in order to connect with the One who is. The more we'll be able to put down our phones and trust God to take care of us when we do.

> Look at the birds. They don't plant or harvest or store food in barns, for your heavenly Father feeds them. And aren't you far more valuable to him than they are?
>
> **MATTHEW 6:26, NLT**

Look up Exodus 34:6 and write it below.

Underline the word *gracious* in the verse.

In your own words, what does it mean to be gracious?

> Let us then approach God's throne of grace with confidence, so that we may receive mercy and find grace to help us in our time of need.
> **HEBREWS 4:16, NIV**

One of my favorite definitions of grace is "getting what you don't deserve." That means grace begins with the borrowed breath in my lungs and keeps going with the food in my fridge, the friends in my life, the forgiveness I receive from Christ. God is a generous God, giving us what we don't deserve all of the time. And when we believe that's true, we can let our defenses down a bit to connect with God's grace in our lives.

So, let's explore grace a little more.

Read Hebrews 4:16.

What is God's throne called?

How can we approach God's throne?

What will we find at God's throne?

When can we come to God's throne?

Gift means grace, and grace means gift. They are synonymous. So when God says we can boldly approach the throne of grace with confidence, we can picture approaching a throne room full of gifts coming from a generous King.

Circle the words *grace* and *gift* in the verses below.

> It is by grace you have been saved, through faith—and this is not from yourselves, it is the gift of God—not by works, so that no one can boast.
> EPHESIANS 2:8-9, NIV

God loves giving good gifts to His children! And one of the best gifts we can find in Him? Connection to our good, gracious Father.

One year my youngest son became completely obsessed with Halloween (as all good second graders do). Once October hit, he was constantly asking questions about when Halloween festivities would start:

"When can we go pick out our pumpkins?"

"When can we carve them?"

"When will we pick out Halloween candy?"

"What will I be for Halloween?"

"When will the costume be ready?"

As a human, I feel "meh" about this holiday. But as his momma, I started to get excited with him. Because while I don't love Halloween, I do love *him*. And because of that love, I wanted to connect with my son over something he loved. So, I started to think, "How can I give him something fun this season? How can I join him in his love for Halloween?"

One evening on the drive home from yet another of his older brother's soccer games, I realized how close we were to the pumpkin farm. I remembered how many times he had asked me in the past three weeks when we could go get our pumpkins and how often I said, "I'm not sure, buddy. We have a lot going on."

I veered left even though my heart wanted to go right home. Because I love my son, and I love to give good gifts to him. As we pulled up to the farm, his face was worth the price of admission. "Are we getting pumpkins now?! Oh thank you, Momma! Thank you! I can't believe today is the day!" My heart swelled. We both smiled the whole time as he inspected many pumpkins and chose the best one. He thanked me the whole way home.

Gift-giving is great fun. And the biggest gift? The connection because of it.

Recall a recent time when your Heavenly Father gave you a gift you didn't expect or deserve—a gift of grace. What gift did God give you? A message from a friend? A new job? A surprise coffee from a coworker?

Write out what it felt like to receive that gift.

If you can't think of a gift you've received like this, write a prayer asking for a gift from His throne.

Staying true to God's declaration of Himself as a gracious God, Jesus Himself embodies grace.

Read John 1:14-17.

What do you find out about grace from this passage regarding Jesus?

If we are going to replace our phones with true connection, what we believe about what that phone will do for us has to be addressed first. Can that phone actually take care of me? Can it provide for me? Or is it better to put my trust in a gracious God who promises to give me more than I can ask for or imagine?

Maybe this seems like a sacrilegious question, but I'm going to ask it nonetheless: *How is God better than your phone?*

If He really is better, what is it that keeps us starving for real connection behind that screen? Why do we keep picking it up, over and over? What is it about our phones that keeps us coming back for more?

Take a minute and journal your thoughts below.

Remember, real nourishment flows from the throne of God. It's there in every gracious gift He gives us. It's there in every aspect of His generous character. If we don't make space to connect with God there, we'll miss it.

And friend, I don't want you to miss it!

THE PRACTICE OF CONNECTION

We ended yesterday with five minutes of silence, and today we will set aside six minutes.

Like yesterday, let's clear everything out of sight for six minutes of silence to connect with God. Turn off any music, television, noise, or screens. Maybe go outside if you can. Remember, those first few minutes may seem as if thought monkeys are coming to take over your brain. Just breathe through them. This is normal. Everything else that comes to mind will be waiting for you when you are done.

Here is a breath prayer to use during your six minutes today if it helps. Inhale for four counts (one word for each count). Exhale for five counts (one word for each count).

Inhale: God, you are gracious.
Exhale: I am in Your care.

How was your time of silence? Record any reflections you have.

PATIENT AS THE DAY IS LONG

If there's one thing as sure as the sunrise, it's that I was born with a short fuse. Mercy. I have been working on my temper, my anger, the unmet expectations underneath my frustration for years. I am grateful that I have come a long way. I have added many tools to my tool belt to use when anger rises, thanks to all of my counselors. They deserve all the coffees and scones and hugs. Because I'm a mess, and they've helped me out of the pit many times.

As we keep exploring whether we can truly put down our phones and find connection to and trust God, we are looking at the description of His character that He proclaimed to Moses—a description that would be repeated and called upon for hundreds of generations.

Underline the third attribute of God's character in our verse for this week.

> He passed in front of Moses, proclaiming, "The LORD, the LORD, the compassionate and gracious God, slow to anger, abounding in love and faithfulness."
>
> **EXODUS 34:6, NIV**

I'm just so incredibly grateful that God made sure we knew that being slow to anger was in His DNA. Because we blow it, over and over. At least I do! Slow to anger isn't a phrase anyone in my family would use to describe me. But it's certainly true of the God we serve. His compassion and grace also lead God to be slow to anger toward us.

I'm grateful we can trust a God who is slow not only in anger, but in timing.

Read the verse below and consider why God is "slow" according to this passage.

> The Lord is not slow to fulfill his promise as some count slowness, but is patient toward you, not wishing that any should perish, but that all should reach repentance.
>
> **2 PETER 3:9**

Fill in the blank.

God is patient toward _____.

God is patient toward *you.*
And me. And all of us.

Why? So that more and more will repent, turn their thinking around, and come to know—to connect—with Him. What a good God! I don't know about you, but I believe I can trust a God who has decided to keep a posture of patience toward me. We can trust a God who is patient with us because He has our best in mind.

Our phones? They don't care who we are. They give us image after image that can cause us to be anxious, to compare, to fix ourselves, to worry. They're starving us of the patience and peace that comes from a patient and peaceful God.

Having a Father who is slow to anger may be something very foreign to you. You may have grown up with a father who was quick to anger, impatient, and full of frustration at the world, or his job, or at you. My dad was quick to be angry when house repair was involved. He was hardly ever quick to be angry at humans, but always at leaky toilets.

No matter what our experience with an earthly father has been, the good news for all of us is this: *God is not our earthly father.*

He is patient.
He is kind.

He is compassionate.

He is gracious.

He is slow to anger.

What comfort does knowing this truth about God's character give you?

Because God is slow to anger, we can rest assured that when we wander away from connection with Him, He longs to restore us and bring us back into fellowship with Him. He doesn't want to destroy us; He wants to redeem us.

When this lesson is applied to us, we love it! But when it extends to other people? Not always as easy. Maybe like me, you've felt like Jonah. You wish God was quicker to anger with others.

Jonah believed the people of Nineveh deserved to be punished for all of their sins. He did not want to bring good news to this city. He thought they were beyond grace. But God saved the people of Nineveh—all 120,000 of them. Take a look at Jonah's response to God after that:

> To Jonah this seemed very wrong, and he became angry. He prayed to the LORD, "Isn't this what I said, LORD, when I was still at home? That is what I tried to forestall by fleeing to Tarshish. I knew that you are a gracious and compassionate God, slow to anger and abounding in love, a God who relents from sending calamity. Now, LORD, take away my life, for it is better for me to die than to live."
> **JONAH 4:1-3, NIV**

What Scripture do you think Jonah was thinking about when he talked about God's character?

I need you to know I have felt like Jonah. Angry that others didn't get the wrath of God. Angry that God wasn't angry enough to punish my enemies. Angry that God didn't do anything to the ones who have betrayed me, hurt me, rejected me, and stolen from me. Angry that God didn't work with a short fuse like me.

If you've been there, congratulations. You are human. Our anger can be an indicator that we are protecting something precious to us. Sometimes what is precious to us needs to be crucified (like our pride), but sometimes it needs to be fiercely honored and guarded (like our dignity). Jesus flipped tables to protect His Father's house as a place of prayer, not commerce. As a place of knowing God, not buying and selling. As a place marked for worship, not for marked-up sacrifices. There, the anger is for the sake of defending what is honorable and good.

But if we can ever so tenderly swivel the camera toward us and our own hearts, I wonder what we will find. If we feel indignant at others for their sins and choices, as Jonah did, are we able to see our own sins and choices in the same light? Are we able to see the anger we may have caused others? All I can hear is Paul in my ears on this one:

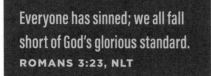

Everyone has sinned; we all fall short of God's glorious standard.
ROMANS 3:23, NLT

All have sinned; all fall short. We could stop there. That should be enough, right?

Well, Paul goes on:

Yet God, in his grace, freely makes us right in his sight. He did this through Christ Jesus when he freed us from the penalty for our sins. For God presented Jesus as the sacrifice for sin. People are made right with God when they believe that Jesus sacrificed his life, shedding his blood.

ROMANS 3:24-25, NLT

Praise!

I know I can be afraid to turn off all the noise and distraction because I might get a wagging finger from God. Maybe I hide behind my phone in order to avoid connecting with God who I fear will greet me with arms folded in disapproval. Maybe I run from a frustrated God who is sighing with impatience at how long I'm taking to grow.

I may do those things, but they're not doing anything for me. In fact, they're starving me from the connection I need—the connection that will remind me who God really is when I meet with Him.

The God who is slow to anger.

Are you afraid of what kind of God you'll get if you disconnect from distractions? How is being silent connected to your view of God and His potential anger toward you?

To end our time today, read Psalm 103:1-19. Write down what you find out about what God the Father is really like.

What if, for today's practice of silence, you imagined God as patient and slow to anger? What is His face like? What are His arms doing? What is His posture like? What is He saying to you?

Connect with that image of God in your mind today. Find nourishment in the presence of a God who is slow to anger.

THE PRACTICE OF CONNECTION

Today, practice seven minutes of silence. I hope this is a freeing and lifegiving experiment for you this week. Put away all distractions. Try to sit by a window or outside. Breathe slowly. Close your eyes and let your imagination build a picture of your good Father, patient and slow to anger.

If it helps, here is a breath prayer you can use during your seven minutes. Inhale for six counts (one word for each count). Exhale for six counts (one word for each count).

> *Inhale: God, you are slow to anger.*
> *Exhale: Father, I am in Your care.*

THE GREAT MINT TAKEOVER

We bought this lovely little dilapidated house a few years into our marriage. Talk about a fixer-upper. It was 2003, so we were way ahead of Chip and Jo on this one. It would take pages for me to tell you about everything that needed to be repaired, restored, and rebuilt. But we were spry and didn't have any children yet, so we went for it. We redeemed that beauty, stained glass and all.

The first time my husband mowed the two-foot-high lawn in the backyard (around the Chronicles of Narnia lamppost sitting dead center in the yard that we never could get working), I expected to get hit with a whiff of fresh-cut grass. But it was quite a different smell. Not a stench, but not the scent of grass either. My husband stopped the mower and we both said, "What's that smell?" The answer hit us both like a strong mojito on a summer day: mint!

Who knew that mint would conquer entire plots of land if you let it? About one third of our yard wasn't grass after all. It was mint. The Great Mint Takeover was well underway, and every neighbor knew it right then. The smell took over the street as soon as we started mowing the lawn. We had a plentiful quantity, enough for a bazillion soups, salads, drinks, and desserts. You might say we were abounding in mint.

That brings us to the fourth characteristic we want to look at from Exodus 34:6. God is "abounding in love."

What do you think of when you hear the word *abounding*?

The dictionary tells us that *abounding* means "existing in or providing a great or plentiful quantity or supply."[1]

And in this case? The supply is LOVE.

Our God is great and plentiful in His love toward you. What a fresh and rich thought, like the smell of mint permeating the air of your neighborhood in place of freshly cut grass. His love is *that* good, that real, that nourishing to our souls.

On a scale of 1 to 10 (1 being God is stingy with His love for you and 10 being God is abounding in His love for you), how do you feel about the way God loves you? Why?

God is stingy with His love　　　　　　**God is abounding in His love**

1　　2　　3　　4　　5　　6　　7　　8　　9　　10

Let's take a look at some places we can see God's love at work, up close and personal.

God demonstrates his own love for us in this: While we were still sinners, Christ died for us.

ROMANS 5:8-10, NIV

How did God demonstrate His own love for us?

How does that act show you God's love is abounding?

Read the verse below about the depth of God's love:

> I have been crucified with Christ and I no longer live, but Christ lives
> in me. The life I now live in the body, I live by faith in the Son of God,
> who loved me and gave himself for me.
> GALATIANS 2:20, NIV

What two verbs are assigned to the Son of God here that directly apply to you?

He _____ me.
He _____ himself for me.

In the smallest way, I can relate. When my oldest son was diagnosed with Crohn's disease in 2018, everything inside of me wished I was the one given the chronic illness. If I could have traded places with him, I would have. I would have taken the disease, the management of food and pain, the overwhelming health and treatment plan to find remission. That's because I love him, and a mother's love for her child is fierce.

But here's the kicker: my son is MINE. He is easy to love, because he's my boy. My precious, amazing, wonderful, brilliant boy. A part of my family. And he's a kid who loves us as much as we love him.

In other words, it's easy to have abounding love for him.

So, let's take in the fact that God loved us when we were not loving to Him. In fact, we are called something else. **Read Romans 5:10 again. What were we according to this verse?**

We were enemies of God. *Enemies.* Let that soak in. An enemy is someone who is against you at every turn, actively opposed or hostile to you. And this is how we were toward God. Going our own way. Living our own life. Going against God's Kingdom way.

No wonder we're starving, friend.

But don't worry, there's still good news here. Though we were born slaves to sin, Jesus set us free from that slavery, and now, we are ruled by the Spirit. Now, we are family to God.

Look how Paul describes this reality:

> Those who are led by the Spirit of God are the children of God. The Spirit you received does not make you slaves, so that you live in fear again; rather, the Spirit you received brought about your adoption to sonship. And by him we cry, "*Abba, Father.*" The Spirit himself testifies with our spirit that we are God's children. Now if we are children, then we are heirs—heirs of God and co-heirs with Christ, if indeed we share in his sufferings in order that we may also share in his glory.
> **ROMANS 8:14-17, NIV**

I love this explanation from *Got Questions*:

Christians are born enslaved, but Jesus buys them out of slavery and they are adopted by the Father and given the Spirit, so now they are heirs.

When we come to faith in Christ, our debts are cancelled, we are given a new name, and we are given all the rights that heirs of God possess. . . . Christians are not adopted because God thinks they will make worthy heirs. God adopts people who are completely unworthy, because He adopts on the basis of His grace.[2]

All of this theology is quite profound, but unless we address the heart along with the head, we won't get anywhere. So, let's get real about this. *I think the hard part about truly believing God's abounding love for us is in the contrast between our own expectation of what His love should look like in our lives and how our lives actually look.*

We have unmet expectations that may have starved us from believing God loves us. We expected God's love to look a certain way. Maybe we expected to be married by now. Or we expected to have children by now. Or we expected to have our dream job by now. Or we expected to be free of traumatic memories by now. Or any number of expectations that we have held against God as proof of His love.

For years we struggled through infertility. And I had to fight tooth and nail to believe in God's love for me. It took me some time to realize I had thought this thought: *God's love equals a baby in my arms.* With that ringing true in my head, the only logical next thought was this: *If I don't have a baby, God must not really love me.*

Thank goodness for God's abounding love to remind me what is actually true. Because in reality, God doesn't demonstrate His love for us by meeting all our expectations in our own way.

In those days, I had to frequently remember this truth based in Romans 5:8: *Jesus demonstrated His love to me by dying for me—not by giving me a child or healing my infertility or working on my timetable.*

Can we get very personal and very honest?

When you think about the unmet expectations that may prevent you from believing in God's abounding love for you, what would your sentence look like?

Here are a few prompts to use:

God's love equals _____ .
Jesus demonstrated His love to me
    by dying for me—not by _____ .

I am going to leave space on the next page for you to process and journal more of what may have come to mind. You may have a lot of pent-up disappointment, anger, or resentment surrounding how you think God ought to demonstrate His love toward you. I've been there, friend! Talk to Him about it.

Write out your honest thoughts and cries. Connect with His abounding love here. *Take your time and reflect here.*

THE PRACTICE OF CONNECTION

Today, we are closing with eight minutes of silence. You can do this! I believe in you, friend. Prepare yourself for this time. Set a timer if you'd like, but then turn your phone over. Find a quiet space. Breathe. If you need a prompt for your silence, consider again the truth about God's love for you. I have emphasized a few truths here:

> What, then, shall we say in response to these things? *If God is for us, who can be against us?* He who did not spare his own Son, but gave him up for us all—how will he not also, along with him, graciously give us all things? . . . *Who shall separate us from the love of Christ?* . . . For I am convinced that neither death nor life, neither angels nor demons, neither the present nor the future, nor any powers, neither height nor depth, *nor anything else in all creation, will be able to separate us from the love of God that is in Christ Jesus our Lord.*
> **ROMANS 8:31-32;35; 38-39, NIV (EMPHASIS ADDED)**

If it helps, here is a breath prayer you can use during your eight minutes. Inhale for five counts (one word for each count). Exhale for five counts (one word for each count).

Inhale: God, you abound in love.
Exhale: I am in your care.

FAITHLESS PHONES, FAITHFUL GOD

So far this week, we have explored that God is compassionate, gracious, slow to anger, and abounding in love. **Underline the final attribute of God's character we are looking at today.**

> He passed in front of Moses, proclaiming, "The LORD, the LORD, the compassionate and gracious God, slow to anger, abounding in love and faithfulness."
>
> **EXODUS 34:6, NIV**

Not only is God overflowing and plentiful in His love for us, but He is abounding in His faithfulness to us too.

In your own words, what does *faithfulness* mean to you?

You may have listed being reliable and steadfast, having integrity, being true to your word, or something to the effect of being unwavering. Good work!

The incredible thing about God's faithfulness is that even when *we* are faithless toward Him, He is faithful to us. We are going to look at Luke 15 to read a story that puts skin on the character of God. Every single one of the attributes we've discovered this week is displayed in this story. Take a deep breath and ask God to show you something about Him you may have never seen before in this parable as you read.

Slowly read Luke 15:11-32.

I have been obsessed with Luke 15:20 for quite some time. I cannot for the life of me get away from it. **Write out the five verbs that are true of the father from Luke 15:20 below:**

1.

2.

3.

4.

5.

> He got up and went to his father. But while he was still a long way off, his father saw him and was filled with compassion for him; he ran to his son, threw his arms around him and kissed him. **LUKE 15:20, NIV**

If this is not a manifestation of Exodus 34:6, then I don't know what is! Let's compare notes here:

In Exodus 34:6, these are the attributes of God:

- Compassionate
- Gracious
- Slow to anger
- Abounding in love
- Abounding in faithfulness

In Luke 15:20, these are the actions of the father:

- Sees his son
- Is filled with compassion for him
- Runs toward the son
- Embraces his son
- Kisses his son

What a gift to see the consistency of the character of God across thousands of years. *From Exodus to Luke, God is the same.* Jesus told this story because the Pharisees were mad that He was associating with notorious sinners—eating with them even! He wanted them to know that God's love was faithful to *all* of us. He wanted them to be fed by that truth, and I think He wants the same for us as we read it today.

But maybe you are like a young woman I recently talked to at a retreat where I was speaking. She felt much more like the older, faithful son who had done everything right and served his father endlessly. She felt left behind and unwanted. She was frustrated since it seemed the new believers who have shady pasts get to be celebrated and honored while those like her are looked over and forgotten. After we spoke about this late one night, I had to go back to the passage to see how the father in this story responds to his other son.

Look again at Luke 15:31. What does the father say? Write it out here:

I wrote this verse on a piece of paper and passed it to the woman at the retreat before I spoke. I felt like God wanted her to have a personal note to remind her of the truth: God sees her, and everything He has is hers.

God is faithful to us all.

I love that, like the father in the parable, God says, "Everything I have is yours." It's as if He says, "I am just as generous, and compassionate, and gracious, and slow to anger, and abounding in love and faithfulness to you as I am to your brother. EVERYTHING I HAVE IS YOURS. I am not sparing one thing. For the faithful and the unfaithful, my compassionate grace will cover every one of you."

God's faithfulness is abounding. And that's true for us all. No matter what we've done, how we've starved ourselves from connection with God, or how we've attemped to find that connection in our phones or anywhere else, the good news of this week is that we can trust the character of God. We can trust Him to care for us. We can trust Him to love us. We can trust Him to handle us with patience and grace. We can trust Him to be faithful. We can trust Him to feed us.

Well, we have had quite a week exploring the character of God. And we've gone even further, putting down our phones and picking up true connection to God in our silence.

How has putting down your phone, practicing silence, and meditating on God's character helped you find true connection this week? What has been hard? What has been good?

For me, one of the things I've found so interesting is learning what I'm asking my phone to do for me.

My phone is not compassionate. In fact, I find it can be a real source of shame for me in a variety of ways, like comparison, envy, jealousy, and not measuring up.

My phone is not gracious. It cannot give me spiritual gifts or free me from my sin.

My phone is not slow to anger or abounding in love or abounding in faithfulness. In fact, my phone can make me quick to anger when it breeds comparison, frustration, and more.

And though my phone is always there, it cannot provide lasting peace or enduring comfort. It cannot provide for me or give me life.

Not like my faithful God can.

I hope this week has given you a taste for building the practice of silence into your lives. We are starving for a soul connection to our Creator. He made us and wants to tell us all about Himself, all about who He made us to be, all about what He has for us to do. He wants to feed our souls through His presence and to teach us how to trust His character in the silence. Part of this practice is to remove all distractions so we can enjoy our connection to Him.

This week we truly practiced a three-part remedy:

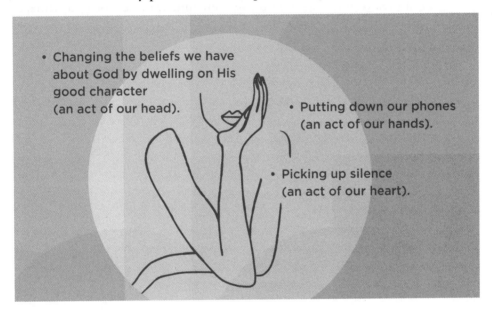

- Changing the beliefs we have about God by dwelling on His good character (an act of our head).

- Putting down our phones (an act of our hands).

- Picking up silence (an act of our heart).

Even if this week felt terribly hard, uncomfortable, or unfamiliar to you, what are you taking away with you?

THE PRACTICE OF CONNECTION

We will close our week with nine whole delicious minutes of silence. To prepare for this time, take a moment to do a brain dump! Write as much as you can as quickly as you can, filling the space below with all the thoughts or things you have to do or the worries on your mind. Dump it out. It will be there after your intentional connection with God. Now, find a good spot to breathe and enjoy God's presence.

Here is a breath prayer to use during your nine minutes today if it helps. Inhale for four counts (one word for each count). Exhale for five counts (one word for each count).

Inhale: God, feed my soul.
Exhale: I am in Your care.

DAD'S FAMOUS CHICKEN STRIPS

Something happens around our kitchen bar just about every Monday night. When my kids start to smell frying chicken, all of a sudden everyone gets really close to one another, huddled in the kitchen. All five of us end up standing around snacking on chicken strips, laughing, sharing, and connecting. Because good food does that. It brings us together, lowers our guard, opens our hearts. I've heard that it's hard to eat at a table with a sword in your hand. May these chicken strips bring all the connection and all the satisfied bellies.

Ingredients

2 eggs
2½ lbs. chicken strips
1½ cups almond flour
½ cup oat flour
1 tsp. garlic powder

½ tsp. onion powder
1½ tsp. salt
¼ tsp. pepper
olive oil to cook in

Instructions

1. Beat eggs in a medium bowl. Combine egg mixture and chicken pieces in the bowl, stirring until all pieces are covered with egg mixture. Drain excess egg off chicken using a strainer.

2. Combine all dry ingredients (almond flour through pepper) in a small bowl, and then sprinkle on top of drained chicken in a medium bowl. Stir gently until all the pieces are covered.

3. Add about ¼ inch of oil to a medium saucepan placed over medium-high heat. Once the oil is hot and begins to shimmer, place coated chicken strips in the oil. Don't overcrowd the pan—there should be space between the pieces.

4. Cook for 5-6 minutes on each side, until crispy golden brown. Repeat until all pieces are cooked through, with no pink inside. We use a kitchen thermometer to make sure each strip is cooked to 165°F.

5. Serve with dipping sauces of your choice, such as ketchup, honey mustard, or our family favorite: Primal Kitchen Buffalo Sauce.

Note that the recipes in this book are compliant for our family's unique dietary needs. We have used the SCD diet (specific carbohydrate diet) and the book *Breaking the Vicious Cycle* by Elaine Gottschall for Crohn's disease.

STARVED BY SHAME

Questions for Discussion

THE PROBLEM
What is starving us in our desire to be loved?

THE PROMISE
What Scriptures have been feeding your soul lately?

THE PRACTICE
What spiritual practices can satiate you when your soul is starved for love?

PERSONAL REFLECTION
Choose a question and take a moment to journal your response.

- What is a recurring shame story that plays in the back of your mind?
- What are the five verbs given to describe the Father in the story of the Prodigal Son in Luke 11? Which one speaks to you right now?
- If you could tell yourself a one-sentence story about being God's beloved, what would it be?

Video sessions available for download at amyseiffert.com.

STARVED BY SHAME

To get the most out of this week's study, read chapter 2 of *Starved*.

ALL BY MYSELF

A friend called and invited me to her place. She's a younger friend with a two-year-old child, so she is certainly in the weeds of diapers, naps, and sippy cups. I am in the throes of high school, soccer practice, and the nighttime taxi. She's young in her faith, and I love to spend time with her, though we live about forty minutes apart.

But I have to admit, when the only way we could meet was for me to drive to her place, I wrestled with it. I wrestled because I struggle with believing in God's abundance when it comes to my time. I have been working on overcoming a scarcity mindset about things like time, resources, and energy. If I drove up and back and spent time with her in between, would I be able to get the other things done on my list? Like write this Bible study?

And then, I sensed a nudge. The kind of elbow to the rib only the Holy Spirit can give you. What if I set aside the drive up there for intentional solitude? What if this driving time now in my schedule for the day was consecrated to listening to the good story God has for me? What if I turned off the podcasts and the music and took this natural space in my day to be with God? What if I asked God to recover any shame I have? What if I allowed God to use that forty minutes in the car all by myself to help me remember I am His beloved?

The thing is, *we are never alone*. Jesus is always with us. *Always*. But if we never actually practice being just with Jesus, the noise may be deafening. Maybe you even experienced this last week during our practice of silence.

This week's practice may feel similar, but it has one different element to it. We will practice solitude—which is different from silence. Solitude may include silence, but it doesn't have to. But coupled with solitude, we are going to practice story replacement—being alone with God, replacing our shame with our belovedness.

If I'm being honest, I didn't really want to do this during that car ride. As a mom and a wife, I am never alone. It just comes with the territory. So, with precious time in the car all by myself, I didn't really want to give it up. But then, I thought of you. You, sweet friend, doing this study. And I want to be in this with you; I want to do this together. So, I am experimenting with you. Every step of the way. Because if I am going to write about replacing my shame with being God's beloved and using the practice of solitude to do so, you better believe I am going to practice it too.

So off I went on my drive to my friend's house.

I find that I have to start by naming all the initial thought monkeys running around.

God, help me to remember to schedule my children's dentist appointment.

Help me to remember to add olive oil to the grocery list.

Help me to remember to call my friend back.

Help me to think about You, God.

And about who You say I am.

Then, I can listen. I can focus. I can see what God has for me.

My route took me on one of the most beautiful roads in Ohio in the fall. Because I had shut down all the noise, I felt all of my senses brighten. The colors on the trees as I drove were more brilliant to me. The sky was bluer. The clouds were fluffier.

I felt my soul slow down.

And once I can slow down and focus, my mind, my heart, and my soul begin to rest in the practice of solitude with God by my side.

Friend, I hope the same for you this week! Don't beat yourself up for not being good at solitude. Experiment and play with it. Find the natural pauses in your day this week to intentionally listen to God.

As we practice solitude, we want to practice turning our minds to the good story that God has given us. To His nature and posture toward us. To who we are in Jesus. To all the goodness that comes with being a son or daughter of the King.

We are starving for an identity that sets us free from the need to perform, to perfect, to prove. We are so thirsty to hear from God about who we are. And He is ready to give us good gifts. He is calling us to His banquet table of love, joy, and peace.

May this week be a gift to you. One of unwrapping your good and holy birthright of being His beloved. One that reminds you that you're never really alone.

WHERE CYPRESS TREES GROW

Let's start today by opening up the Bible together. **Read Isaiah 55:1-13. Below, write down the verse that stands out to you the most in the passage.**

Now, fill in the blanks according to verse 3 (NLT).

> Come to me with your _____ wide open. Listen, and you will find _____. I will make an _____ covenant with you. I will give you all the _____ love I promised David.

God is calling us to take the time to shut it all down. He's asking us to pay attention. To listen. To move toward Him. To take in the goodness He has for us. God is calling us to come with our ears open. To listen so we find life. He has an everlasting covenant with us and unfailing love, just like He promised David.

And friends, that's amazing news! It's life-giving, nourishing news. But if we have access to this kind of love, why are we still starving?

For me (and likely for you, too), the answer is shame. *We are starved by shame.*

I don't know what shame story is in your life right now. I don't know what is starving you from the love God wants to put in place of that shame. Maybe it's something said to you years ago that keeps defining you and haunting you. Maybe it's past abuse, past hurt, past pain. Maybe it's a broken relationship that you are grieving or a hard word said to you in jest.

No, I don't know when shame began to seep its way into your story. But what I do know is this: *God is calling you to come with ears wide open so He can replace whatever is starving you with His nourishment and life.* He is calling us to listen, so we might find life. Jesus Himself promised this when He said, "The thief comes only to steal and kill and destroy. I came that they may have life and have it abundantly" (John 10:10).

Go back and read Isaiah 55:12-13 again.

I was really struck by the wording of verse 13: "Where once there were thorns, cypress trees will grow" (NLT).

God desires to replace our thorn-stories with cypress-stories. Cypress trees are evergreen conifers known for their use in shipbuilding, wood floors, and musical instruments. They are also known for their medicinal and healing qualities, and in ancient times, many "believed that, as they were always green and pointed towards heaven, they could help souls to rise upwards, which is why they are so often planted in cemeteries."[1]

As we close today, has something that causes shame come to mind? Is there a narrative you believe about yourself that you want God to replace? What are the places you want to hide or cover up? What do you feel shame about in your story? If you're comfortable, write what comes to mind here:

THE PRACTICE OF SOLITUDE

This week we will intentionally practice solitude and story replacement. Today, choose a natural pause you have in your day that you could dedicate to the Lord. A few options for me include things like a car ride, a walk, my lunch hour, or the quiet before bed.

Write down what slot of time you would like to dedicate to the Lord to be alone, just you and Him.

Determine today to spend that time alone with God. As you do so, ask God to replace any shame you have with the knowledge that you are His beloved.

A sample prayer to begin:

God, there are thorns in my life that I want You to dig up and replace with strong, evergreen, healing cypress trees. Show me what those thorns are. Bring healing to those places that are sharp, that continue to starve out the life You've given me. Replace my shame with the knowledge that I am Your beloved. Amen.

THE MAIN COURSE

Every day we wake up, and, either consciously or not, we are ravenous to validate ourselves. Under everything we do, the questions swirl:

Am I liked?

Am I acceptable?

Am I good?

Am I enough?

Am I beautiful?

Am I strong?

Am I worthy?

Am I doing a good job?

Am I invited?

Am I wanted?

Am I an imposter?

Am I capable?

The questions could go on. **Do you have any you would add to the list above?**

The solution for our starving souls is to practice coming to our Creator often. To have Him tell us who we are and Whose we are. To let His truth nourish our aching souls. To climb into His loving lap and listen to Him tell us about how good and compassionate and just and kind He is. To believe Him when

He tells us how delightful and beloved and redeemed and called and wanted we are.

Of course, this doesn't mean we quit our jobs to just hole up and sit with God. It means we come to Him in the middle of those everyday spaces—making a way to hear God in the daily rhythms of our life.

This is why I wanted to start with the call from Isaiah 55 yesterday. He calls us to come and turn our hearts toward God—any which way we can.

He has food for our starving souls.

He has love for our shame-filled hearts.

He has hope for our hopeless spaces.

He has life for our choked-out dreams.

He has food and wine when we have nothing to purchase them with!

Yesterday I wanted us to identify one of the points of shame in our life. Today, I want to share another shame story I wrestle with in my own life.

I often felt in the shadow of my older sister. She was smart and organized while I struggled greatly in school and was often quite messy. Many years later, I was diagnosed with ADHD, which explained a lot. In that same season, I read a few articles about how a messy room is actually a sign of creativity and innovation. Won't I take that narrative instead? Creativity! As I put together a great outfit, my closet would explode in the process. So would my bathroom counter. And well, let's be real, my entire room took a hit every time I got dressed. I was a blank canvas in the making, forgetting all about the colorful and chaotic trail of clothes and accessories behind me. Now, I like to think of that as my creativity at work!

But even with the explanations, the shadow of shame loomed over me. It caused performance and perfectionism issues for me as an adult. I want to look put together, organized, and smart, which means a lot of hustling for my worth, a lot of making sure everything in my life is presenting well (children included—which is what really unraveled me when I became a mom, because it's an impossible mission to keep your children perfect), and a lot of exhaustion. It's tiring to work so hard to try to please everyone, to look good, to stay put together—and all for what? My soul can still starve even if my hair and house look picture perfect.

There's a moment in the Bible I want to look at where nourishment is at stake in several ways. You may be very familiar with this moment in Scripture, so I have included the translation from The Message version here.

> As they continued their travel, Jesus entered a village. A woman by the name of Martha welcomed him and made him feel quite at home. She had a sister, Mary, who sat before the Master, hanging on every word He said. But Martha was pulled away by all she had to do in the kitchen. Later, she stepped in, interrupting them. "Master, don't you care that my sister has abandoned the kitchen to me? Tell her to lend me a hand."
>
> The Master said, "Martha, dear Martha, you're fussing far too much and getting yourself worked up over nothing. One thing only is essential, and Mary has chosen it—it's the main course, and won't be taken from her."
>
> **LUKE 10:38-42, MSG**

Let's really observe this story. If this seems like I'm holding your hand with these questions, I am. Because I want us to really see it all.

When Jesus arrived, how did Martha make Him feel?

What was Mary hanging on?

What was Martha pulled away by?

What did Jesus say was the main course?

Countless books, Bible studies, and sermons have covered this very interaction between Mary, Martha, and Jesus. And honestly, Martha usually gets a bad rap. But what I love here is Martha's bravery and boldness. She bravely asks if God cares about everything that is left for her to do. Then, she boldly asks for what she needs.

I can often play the victim in my own story, slamming pots and pans all around the kitchen so that someone might notice how hard I am working, come praise me, and offer me help. Have you tried this? This method has hardly yielded the great fruit I wanted—if ever.

But Martha feels her frustration rise and comes right to Jesus. Those are some good practices: noticing feelings and coming to Jesus.

If I were to apply this to my own shame story, I would find myself coming up to Jesus and saying things like this:

Don't You see how hard I am working to keep everything together?
Don't You care that I am working my rear off to be loved?
To win everyone over IN YOUR NAME?
To be the best I can be for YOUR kingdom and YOUR glory?

I imagine I might get a tender smile back, along with the same answer He gave Martha.

How often are we doing something God is not asking of us? How often have we taken on a task, a job, a relationship, a service, or an identity that He has not given us? How often have we decided we need to do or be something Jesus isn't calling us to do or be? What if He is asking us to put down the to-do list? To stop with the proving, the pushing, the perfectionism, the obsessive organizing, the overposting on social media, the addiction? What if He's calling us to walk away from what isn't nourishing to our soul?

Is there something you are doing right now that God may not have asked you to do? Something you are using to prove your worth? Something born out of your shame?

Back to the story, Jesus says that being with Him is the main course. How often have I reduced my time with Jesus to a quick handful of chocolate chips from the pantry?

I don't believe Jesus is asking us to sit there all day in a quiet time with our Bibles open. I think He is asking to be the main course in our moments throughout the day. He's saying,

Come to me . . .
In the middle of your workday,
your kitchen, your car,
your errands.
Taste and see that I am the Bread of Life.

Part of allowing Jesus to nourish our souls is to consider how beloved we are. We will dive deeper into the meaning of that word *beloved* tomorrow, but for now, let's end our time today by looking at some Scriptures below. Take with you what you need for your time of solitude today by underlining what is speaking to you as you read.

Now, this is what the LORD, your Creator says, O Jacob,
And He who formed you, O Israel,

"Do not fear, for I have redeemed you [from captivity];
I have called you by name; you are Mine!"
ISAIAH 43:1, AMP

He led me to a place of safety;
   he rescued me because he delights in me.
PSALM 18:19, NLT

The Lord your God is in your midst,
   a mighty one who will save;
he will rejoice over you with gladness;
   he will quiet you by his love;
he will exult over you with loud singing.
ZEPHANIAH 3:17

Behold, a voice from heaven said, "This is my beloved Son, with whom
I am well pleased."
MATTHEW 3:17

As the Father has loved me, so have I loved you. Now remain in my love.
JOHN 15:9, NIV

THE PRACTICE OF SOLITUDE

We'll continue carving out time for solitude with God this week.

To start, write down when and where you will practice that solitude today.

From the verses we covered today, if you had to pick one word to take with you to replace your shame story during some solitude, what word would it be?

A sample prayer to begin:

God, I give You my shame. I know You will replace this old story with a new one—one that gives me life. I ask that You remind me that I am Your beloved. Because of that, there's nothing I need to do or be to be nourished. I can simply rest in who I am and whose I am. Amen.

BELOVED? REALLY?

This week, as we ask God to replace our shame with the truth of being His beloved, we have to admit something to start:

Beloved is a weird word.

No one actually uses it in regular conversation today. It's not like you and I are running around calling one another "beloved." It smacks of Shakespeare and puffy-sleeved costumes.

So, what does it mean?

In your own words, write down what you think of when you hear the word *beloved.*

I love this definition from author and leader Rod Edmondson:

> The word *beloved* . . . literally means "beloved, esteemed, dear, favorite, worthy of love." It's a word indicating an action on the part of the one doing the loving. The God of the universe, the same God who paints a sunset, shapes a mountain and plans the waves at the beach, has chosen to love us, not because of who we are, but because of who He is. Our role in this is to BE-LOVED.[1]

Underline which part of this definition stands out to you. Then, write down why in the space below.

I underlined this sentence: *"It's a word indicating an action on the part of the one doing the loving."* Being beloved is about God, not us. This is about His adoration, delight, joy, and pride in the ones He created in His own, very good image! Being beloved truly has nothing to do with us, our merit, our awards, our promotions, our abilities, our anything. We just exist, and God enjoys us.

The word "favorite" really strikes me in this definition as well. If you have a favorite friend, she is someone you love to do everything and anything with. To laugh, eat, play, cry, sit . . . whatever it is, you'll do it with her by your side. Why? Because she's your favorite, and you feel at home with her. You are free to be yourself in her presence, fully loved and accepted.

Being beloved is so much richer because it has everything to do with God. It is related to agape—a love that has zero conditions. There is nothing you can do to earn God's love, and nothing you can do to lose it. As Edmondson points out, being beloved is just that: BE-LOVED.

When you think of what you have been called, what names have been given to you that are the opposite of beloved? This might be painful, but it matters. We are calling out the shame and writing love all over it. **So, write out names or phrases that have stuck with you and starved you from your dignity.**

My list?
- Flaky
- Flat-chested
- Messy
- Forgetful
- Stupid

Depending on the day, all kinds of lies that I feast upon can keep me starved from the truth of being God's beloved. But Jesus is the Way, the Truth, and the Life (John 14:6). He came to set us free and to nourish our souls with all three—His way, His truth, and His life.

As a Type 3 on the Enneagram, my basic fear is being worthless, and my basic desire is to feel valuable and worthwhile. Awesome. I'm a barrel of fun. If you don't know your Enneagram Type, I recommend checking out the Enneagram Institute to start.[2] If you know your Enneagram Type, you might want to refresh yourself on your basic fear and basic desire. They can unlock a lot of what keeps you from believing you are the beloved.

As a Type 3, I am "ambitious, competent, and energetic," but I can also be "status-conscious and highly driven for advancement." I can be "diplomatic and poised, but can also be overly concerned with . . . image and what others think."[3] I "typically have problems with workaholism and competitiveness."

Sigh.

When I am healthy, I don't feel these fears as often. But when I am not, watch out, world. I will work for my worth until I bleed. So, to practice solitude and thinking about being beloved—loved because God created me and loves what He made—this is a big practice for me. I am not naturally bent toward stopping, thinking, and being. But if I want to remember that I am called to BE-LOVED, I must stop in solitude from time to time.

Let's see how this plays out in Jesus' life. Read the two sections of Scripture below.

Then Jesus came from Galilee to the Jordan to John, to be baptized by him. John would have prevented him, saying, "I need to be baptized by you, and do you come to me?" But Jesus answered him, "Let it be so now, for thus it is fitting for us to fulfill all righteousness." Then he consented. And when Jesus was baptized, immediately he went up from the water, and behold, the heavens were opened to him, and he saw the Spirit of God descending like a dove and coming to rest on

him; and behold, a voice from heaven said, "This is my beloved Son, with whom I am well pleased."
MATTHEW 3:13-17

As the Father has loved me, so have I loved you. Now remain in my love.
JOHN 15:9, NIV

What does the Father call Jesus?

How has Jesus loved us?

So, then, what are we called as Jesus is called?

Now flip to Romans 9:25 in your Bible and underline the word "beloved."

Can you do something for me today? Can you go back to the list of names you wrote down and with really large lettering write the word "BELOVED" right over those words? Really mean it, friend. If you can, find a big marker with a thick, inky edge to cover every single lie with the truth of who you are.

The point is for you to see that those things were indeed said to you, but your identity as beloved is greater, bigger, and more important. That's what defines you now. That's what stops your starving. Those other words have love written across them because of the blood of Jesus.

God wants to call you by a new name.

Turn to Isaiah 43:1. What does God call you in this verse?

What does it mean to you that God looks at you with great compassion and delight and calls you "Mine"?

THE PRACTICE OF SOLITUDE

Today, choose a time to be alone with God. A walk, breakfast, car time, coffee—whatever space you have in your day to be quiet in solitude before the Lord.

Write the time you are setting aside here.

If you are looking for a suggestion for how to use that time, worship Jesus as the original Beloved. Then, meditate on the fact that you, too, are beloved.

A sample prayer to begin:

God, I praise You because I am not disowned. I am not left in my shame. I am not the sum of every lie, every negative word, every false belief I've carried with me. I belong to You, God. And I am beloved.

BLACK PENS, TENDER PALMS

I spent a few summers in different cities around the world as a college student doing summer missions. When I smell cigarette smoke mingled with hot city pavement on a summer day, I am back in the heart of Guadalajara, Mexico. Something about that combination will put me right back to walking by little chocolate croissant pastry stands and *tortas cubanas* carts—the most delicious toasted ham-and-chicken sandwiches around.

That summer there were about twenty of us young college men and women who spent eight weeks facilitating English clubs and classes. We formed relationships with college students at the University of Guadalajara and practiced our languages together as we talked about God, creation, Jesus, relationships, and love.

One of my friends that summer was really wrestling with her identity. Who was she? Was she a worship leader? Was she an artist? Was she good? Was she loved? Was she special? She was a beautifully gifted singer and leader, but her shame would often keep her insecure and questioning.

On our way to campus one afternoon, I noticed some black, swirly art on her hands. Unsure of what it was, I was hesitant to ask. But as we ate our lunches, curiosity won, so I asked her about the ink on her palms. As she slowly turned her hand over, I saw beautiful calligraphy on her palms surrounded by ivy and flowers. It was slightly faded where her palm creased but her hand read in her own gorgeous lettering: *"Belonging to the Lord."*

She said it reminded her that she belongs to God. That when she felt lost, she turned her hand over, and she was found. She has a place in the Kingdom of God. She is wanted. She belongs.

I admired her tenacity to take pen to palm and mark her identity. Shame wants to tell us we are forsaken. And if that's the only soundtrack we play in our minds, it will starve us. But love? Love is where we find nourishment. Love tells us we belong.

Turn your Bible to Isaiah 44:1-5. Read those verses and underline anything that is a good and positive promise in this passage.

My friend was so parched when it came to knowing her identity. Her heart often felt like a dry, cracked, brittle landscape in need of the Spirit of God to water her soul. And friends, can't we all relate?

In this passage, God says He will *"pour water on the thirsty land, and streams on the dry ground."* And my dear friend participated with the Spirit of God on this one—writing the truth on her hand, scrawling the truth on her dry soul— just like Isaiah said some Israelites would do. They would remember Whose they were any which way they could, inky palms and all.

So, let's give this a try. Is there a truth you need to remember in place of your shame? If you can, write that on your hand (or somewhere you'll see it routinely) today.

As we practice replacing our shame stories with the story of being beloved, I've written some contrasting thoughts here for us. **Underline what shame-thinking you most often participate in and then what beloved-thinking you would like to practice instead.**

SHAME-THINKING:
I am not worthy of love.
I am bad.
I am a failure.
I am too flawed to be accepted.
I am judged and condemned.
I am unwanted.

BELOVED-THINKING:

I am created with inherent dignity, value, and
worth by a God who loves what He made.

I am loved.

I am a growing, learning, and changing
human being.

I am flawed and cherished.

I am free from judgment, and there is now
no condemnation for this in Christ Jesus.

I belong to the Lord.

> Shame says that because I am flawed, I am unacceptable. Grace says that though I am flawed, I am cherished. **MICHELLE GRAHAM**

Now, create your own list. On one side of this space, write the shame-thinking you're prone to. Then, on the other side, write the beloved-thinking you'd like to nourish your mind with instead.

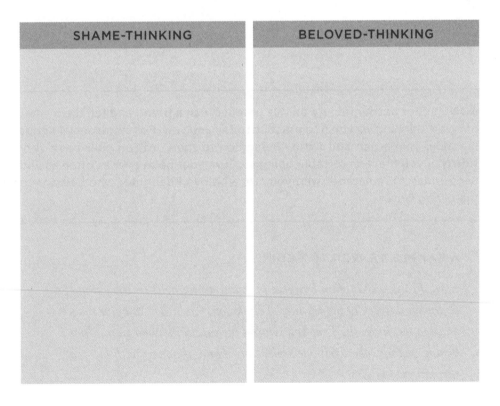

SHAME-THINKING	BELOVED-THINKING

Take a moment to journal a few thoughts on replacing your shame-thinking with beloved-thinking. What would you like to be true of how you think about yourself?

THE PRACTICE OF SOLITUDE

Determine when you would like to practice solitude with God today and write it below. Choose one phrase from your beloved-thinking to focus on today.

BONUS: For accountability on this practice, call a friend and tell them what beloved-thinking you plan to practice today and why. For extraspecial bonus practice, take a pen and write "Belonging to the Lord" on your palm very slowly, if you feel comfortable doing so. Turn your palm over as often as you need today to remember who you are: a beloved daughter who belongs to the Living God.

A SAMPLE PRAYER TO BEGIN:

Lord, I confess that often I give in to shame-thinking. I let those thoughts be the soundtrack of my identity. Thank You, God, that You give me a place to rest in truth. That You remind me constantly who I am. That I belong in Your love. Help me replace my shame-thinking with beloved-thinking today. Amen.

UNMASKING THE WORLD FOR WHAT IT IS

Life of the Beloved is such a short, beautiful, encouraging book on Whose we are. The author, Henri Nouwen, is a master at describing the root issues of our starvation and helping us remember that God has a truth about us that He wants to keep in front of us. Being the beloved is mantel worthy, deserving front and center stage in the living room of our heart. I love the way Nouwen puts it here:

> First of all, you have to keep unmasking the world about you for what it is: manipulative, controlling, power-hungry, and, in the long run, destructive. The world tells you many lies about who you are, and you simply have to be realistic enough to remind yourself of this. Every time you feel hurt, offended, or rejected, you have to dare to say to yourself: "These feelings, strong as they may be, are not telling me the truth about myself. The truth, even though I cannot feel it right now, is that I am the chosen child of God, precious in God's eyes, called the Beloved from all eternity, and held safe in an everlasting embrace."[1]

A real effort must be made to push aside and silence the voices that question our identity. We are *imago Dei*, Latin for the "image of God." We are beloved. Cherished. Delightful. Worth dying for. Remembering the truth that nourishes us is what this Bible study is about, so let's do that today.

Last week, we focused on God's character. This week we've focused on who we are *because* of God's character. Let's finish our week by taking time to look at several places in Scripture that surround and support the idea of being God's beloved.

Before you begin, take a deep breath.

Be slow about this.

This is not a race.

This is not a to-do list to check off.

This is not going to be graded.

This is your identity.

This is your truth that squelches the enemy's lies.

This is security in the face of insecurity.

This is nourishment for what has starved us.

This matters and deserves a slowness that you may not be used to.

I have done many Bible studies where I have fallen behind on my days and found myself rushing through the content so that I could show up to my group with it done. But what is the point? Done for what? For who? This is for you, friend. For your flourishing. For your shield to extinguish the fiery darts of the evil one that come flying at you all day long. Don't rush this. Enjoy each Scripture.

Read each passage now. Then, use the space below each one to reflect on and record your thoughts.

You are treasured.

You are the children of the LORD your God. Do not cut yourselves or shave the front of your heads for the dead, for you are a people holy to the LORD your God. Out of all the peoples on the face of the earth, the LORD has chosen you to be his treasured possession.

DEUTERONOMY 14:1-2, NIV

Reflect:

You are unique. No one else is created like you; no one else has your fingerprint.

You created my inmost being;
   you knit me together in my mother's womb.

PSALM 139:13, NIV

Reflect:

You have good work to do as a masterpiece of God.

We are God's masterpiece. He has created us anew in Christ Jesus, so we can do the good things he planned for us long ago.

EPHESIANS 2:10, NLT

Reflect:

You are redeemed by Christ.

Christ redeemed us from the curse of the law by becoming a curse for us—for it is written, "Cursed is everyone who is hanged on a tree."

GALATIANS 3:13, ESV

Reflect:

You have the resources to make it through anything.

Actually, I don't have a sense of needing anything personally. I've learned by now to be quite content whatever my circumstances. I'm just as happy with little as with much, with much as with little. I've found the recipe for being happy whether full or hungry, hands full or hands empty. Whatever I have, wherever I am, I can make it through anything in the One who makes me who I am.

PHILIPPIANS 4:11-13, MSG

Reflect:

You are God's friend.

I no longer call you servants, because a servant does not know his master's business. Instead, I have called you friends, for everything that I learned from my Father I have made known to you.

JOHN 15:15, NIV

Reflect:

You are forgiven. When past sin is called to mind, this is not from God.

His unfailing love toward those who fear him
   is as great as the height of the heavens above the earth.
He has removed our sins as far from us
   as the east is from the west.

PSALM 103:11-12, NLT

Reflect:

You are a citizen of heaven, not of this world.

Our citizenship is in heaven. And we eagerly await a Savior from there, the Lord Jesus Christ.
PHILIPPIANS 3:20, NIV

Reflect:

Your past does not define you because you are a new creation.

If anyone is in Christ, the new creation has come: The old has gone, the new is here!
2 CORINTHIANS 5:17, NIV

Reflect:

You have the power to overcome fear and worry.

The Spirit God gave us does not make us timid, but gives us power, love and self-discipline.
2 TIMOTHY 1:7, NIV

Reflect:

THE PRACTICE OF SOLITUDE

Determine when you would like to practice solitude with God today and write it below.

What word, idea, or verse do you want to concentrate on today to replace your shame story?

For me, I am taking the idea that I have the resources to make it through anything. I want to practice being content when my hands are empty or full, because I have everything I need in Jesus.

A sample prayer to begin:

Father, thank You for giving us the truth to replace the lies that shame speaks over us. Unmask those in us. Give us eyes to see and ears to hear Your truth in real, lasting ways. Nourish us as Your beloved because that is who we are. Amen.

ROBBY'S GRANOLA BARS

There's no shame in this game. These granola bars are super quick and easy, and they hit all the sweet and salty cravings. They will quickly become just as beloved in your house as you are to Jesus. I'm not kidding—we make these at least twice a week.

Ingredients

½ cup butter
1 cup honey
1 tbsp. vanilla
2 cups oats
¼ cup cashews, roughly chopped

¼ cup unsweetened shredded coconut
¼ cup dried strawberries or banana chips, crushed
¼ cup pecans, roughly chopped

Instructions

1. Line a 9 × 9 baking dish with parchment paper.
2. Bring butter and honey to a boil in a large saucepan. Reduce heat to medium for 3–4 minutes until the syrup turns golden brown. Remove from stove and add vanilla.
3. Stir in the rest of the ingredients until everything is coated in the syrup. If the mixture looks too runny, add more oats.
4. Scoop granola mixture into the prepared pan, press flat, and let cool for about 20 minutes. Slice and watch how fast they go!

STARVED FOR SABBATH

Questions for Discussion

THE PROBLEM
What is starving us in our desire to experience rest?

THE PROMISE
What Scriptures have been feeding your soul lately?

THE PRACTICE
What spiritual practice can satiate you when your soul is starved for rest?

PERSONAL REFLECTION
Choose a question and take a moment to journal.

- What do you believe about God and yourself that keeps you from resting? Really dig deep and uncover what you believe.
- How is resting tied to trusting God?
- Have you ever practiced keeping a sabbath? If so, what has that experience been like for you? What do you like about it? What is hard about it? If not, what has held you back from keeping a sabbath?

STARVED FOR SABBATH

To get the most out of this week's study, read chapter 6 of *Starved*.

A DREAMY DAY

Several years ago, I took a class called Everyday Spirituality taught by Paul Stevens at Regent College. One of the assignments involved investigating the Sabbath. A life-shaping book I read in that time was *Keeping the Sabbath Wholly* by Marva Dawn. In it, she writes:

> In our culture, which attaches such a grand importance to work and productivity, our weekly ceasing reminds us that the value of work lies not in itself nor in the worth it gives us, but in the worship of God that takes place in it. The Sabbath, then, is a sign of liberation. . . . Jesus never called anyone to work. Rather, Jesus calls each one of us to the vocation of following him and of glorifying God in every dimension of our lives. . . .
>
> Our Sabbath keeping is also truly delightful especially because the very process of ceasing from work uncorks our spontaneity and frees our childlike ability to play. Certainly we have all observed that in our society individuals have tremendously deep needs for play. Worries about the stock market and our economic security, fears about climbing the corporate ladder, anxieties about our children or parents or siblings, griefs about our failures and disappointments, frustrations about our limitations . . . —these things frequently rob us of the delight of play. There is something tremendously freeing about knowing we don't have any work to do on the Sabbath. . . .
>
> Freedom to play is a direct result of ceasing work.[1]

Never had I considered what an entire twenty-four hours dedicated to recovering, remembering, and releasing my cares to the Lord would do for me. I had not considered that I had forgotten how to play. I had not considered that Jesus wants to free me from work and instead bring me to worship. In this production-driven, accomplishment-oriented, consumerism-centered view of life we have in the West, I imagine it might do the same for you, too.

The idea that we're allowed, encouraged, and invited to stop striving and rest in God's abundance sounds dreamy, doesn't it? To enjoy play, to put all our cares aside, to stop the striving and hustling we do all week, to connect with God in this Sabbath time.

Yes, it does sound like a dreamy day.

But can we be honest here? It also sounds impossible.

Who can actually stop for an entire day? How does that actually work? What about my young kids? What about soccer games? What about the chores? What about my job? What about the things I need to do to prepare for the week? For my family? My husband? Myself?

With these thoughts in mind, all of a sudden, the Sabbath feels like a burden. An impossible mark to hit. Another bar set too high.

This is why I loved Marva Dawn's book on this practice of Sabbath so much. Reading it opened up a different conversation—a different set of questions.

What if Sabbath was courage? The courage to keep going for six days strong, knowing you have an entire day to cease striving and rest?

What if Sabbath was permission? Permission to stop believing the universe revolves around you and trust God to provide for you?

What if Sabbath was freedom? Freedom from seeing everyone according to their accomplishments? From seeing yourself on a measuring stick sometimes higher, sometimes lower?

What if Sabbath was a gift to be unwrapped? Not a burden to shoulder but a prize to be savored?

I believe Sabbath is all of those things and more. It doesn't have to just sound dreamy; it can actually be the things we long for it to be. But friends, to know that, we have to practice it. We have to experience it. We have to make time to Sabbath.

Because we are starving for it.

Maybe you intentionally rest each week, and this is old news to you. Or maybe you've considered setting aside a day to Sabbath, but you've never actually done it. Maybe you've been unsure of what to do or even how to do it. Let me encourage you, friend: you will not regret it one bit if you Sabbath. By the end of this week, you will have all you need to give it a go.

And I want you to give it a go! I want you to find nourishment in this sacred practice. Though it isn't always easy to do, the effort we put in to set aside the time for Sabbath will be well worth it. I know, because I've experienced it myself.

So together, let's commit to giving it a try this week. Let's commit together to finding nourishment in all that Sabbath offers us.

DAY 1

A SHEPHERD FOR OUR SABBATH

To begin this week, let's get real about rest by answering a few questions together.

Why don't we rest?

What keeps us busy?

Why do we just keep going, filling up our calendars, hurrying around, running our kids ragged, and acting very important?

For me, busy is safe.

Busy is meaningful.

Busy is important.

Busy is an identity.

Busy covers up fear.

I am afraid if I rest, I won't be important.

I'm afraid if I rest, I won't like what I find in the quiet.

I'm afraid if I rest, I won't be loved and admired.

Busy certainly isn't a fruit of the Spirit. In fact, keeping in step with the

Spirit may not look like busyness at all. As Paul tells us, the result of walking alongside the Spirit of God is this: love, joy, peace, patience, kindness, goodness, faithfulness, gentleness, , and self-control. When I am carrying others' opinions with resentment, I don't often look like what Paul describes.

Turn to 2 Timothy 1:7 and write it out below:

God has *NOT* given us a spirit of fear, that's true. But fear doesn't have to be wasted. Fear can actually be a scout for us if we listen. Fear helps us ask important questions:

So, what is it?
What am I afraid of if I just stop?
If I created a rhythm that intentionally includes rest?
If I take the time in silence to renew my mind?
What do I fear if I say no to this next project?
If I clear our calendar?
If I let go of opinions and expectations and rest my heart, mind, and soul?

When we look below the surface, there's more to fear than we realize.

I am afraid I won't be worth anything.
I am afraid I won't be necessary or important.
I am afraid if I don't keep everything running smoothly at high speed,
    then I won't matter.
I am afraid I have to run the world.

This is a lot to carry—an exhausting load. I'm tired just thinking about it. No wonder we're starving, friend!

This is where we need to call upon God's identity and ours. God is compassionate, gracious, slow to anger, abounding in love and faithfulness. And we are His created image-bearers, beloved in His sight, and belonging to Him. He has

> The LORD is my shepherd;
> I have all that I need.
>
> **PSALM 23:1, NLT**

not created us to run ourselves into the ground trying to gain approval, trying to be good, trying to earn our worth. We have His approval. We have His acceptance. He has created us to be in relationship with Him, one in which our soul is in His care—the care of our Good Shepherd.

Read Psalm 23 slowly. Think about how we are God's sheep, and He is our Good Shepherd. Consider the correlation between having a Good Shepherd and practicing the Sabbath, and reflect on it below.

Make a list of all that God provides for you as your Shepherd.

I wanted to take us to Psalm 23 because the linchpin of the Sabbath is trusting God as our Provider. If we rest, He will provide. If we rest, He will renew our strength. If we rest, He will still work.

The first time we see the idea of Sabbath is in the first few pages of the Bible. **Read Genesis 2:1-3. What did God bless?**

God designed the seventh day to be unlike any other day in the week. In the *Starved* book, I talk about the fact that God didn't do this because He was tired. He didn't rest because He ran out of energy. He was putting a rhythm of work and rest into play. Rest is a rhythm He was setting in place for us to follow. He rested not because *He* needs it, but because *we* do.

It's a model of a rhythm that will nourish us as we rest.

THE PRACTICE OF SABBATH

This week we are going to make preparations to be able to practice a Sabbath. By the end of the week, you will have everything you need to trust God to rest.

Many folks set aside either Friday evening through Saturday evening or Saturday evening through Sunday evening for their Sabbath. Choose what works for you! There is no rule or right day to do this, friend.

If you could set a rhythm of work and rest, what day would you set aside to rest?

Preparation is part of keeping the Sabbath. Think of a time when you got ready to go to a special event or on a date. You most likely showered, picked out your outfit, did your hair and makeup, maybe wore perfume. The point is you took time to get yourself ready for a special evening. Consider the Sabbath the same. What would you need to get ready to be able to rest for a day? For me, I take Saturdays to do some house chores, grocery shopping, and meal prep in order to begin resting Saturday evening. When my kids were little, I prepared a little box of toys we only got out on the Sabbath. When they napped on Sundays, so did we. It's what worked for our rhythm.

Write out a few thoughts on preparing to Sabbath this week. If you already practice the Sabbath, write out anything you'd like to change in your preparation.

STOP TRYING AND START TRUSTING

It's exhausting trying to be God. I'm not very good at it. I am not good at orchestrating outcomes. I am not good at keeping everything moving along perfectly. I am not particularly good at making sunrises and sunsets.

Thank goodness we weren't asked to be God, right? Not only would we fail miserably (as we do each time we attempt to play God in our own lives), but we'd run ourselves into the ground. That's because we need rest, friend! Real, deep, trusting rest that stops our starving. The rest that comes from Sabbath.

Marva Dawn gives us four categories to think through for a day of rest. Her Sabbath thoughts fall into these themes: ceasing, resting, embracing, and feasting.[1] Because I've found each one so helpful, we're going to walk through these categories this week. Today, let's start with ceasing.

Ceasing simply means to stop. Stop trying to be God. Stop trying to earn your value. Stop trying to achieve as a measure of your dignity. Just stop.

This makes me think of the words of Jesus when it comes to ceasing the need to be God. Read Matthew 11:28-30. Note what Jesus says He will show us.

Jesus is inviting us to learn the unforced rhythm of grace. It's a rhythm God showed us years ago, way back in Exodus. In fact,

> Are you tired? Worn out? Burned out on religion? Come to me. Get away with me and you'll recover your life. I'll show you how to take a real rest. Walk with me and work with me—watch how I do it. Learn the unforced rhythms of grace. I won't lay anything heavy or ill-fitting on you. Keep company with me and you'll learn to live freely and lightly.
>
> **MATTHEW 11:28-30, MSG**

God had a show-and-tell moment regarding the Sabbath back then. He showed His people how He would provide for them first, before He set it into stone.

Read Exodus 16:1-36. (This is the entire chapter. Enjoy! It gives you the context of God's first provision about the Sabbath to the Israelites.)

According to Exodus 16:12, what is the reason God gives for providing meat and bread?

God wants the Israelites to know that everything—every good and perfect thing—is from His hand. He is God. He is the Provider. He gives food. He gives shelter. He gives everything we need. He is not out to punish us by telling us to stop working. He's out to bless us by giving us rest!

Remember God's character here. He is a gift-giving, compassionate God! He loves to give good gifts to us, His children. Gifts like rest and freedom and food and security and joy. Gifts meant to nourish and satisfy our starving souls.

Some wonderful research has come out about mindsets and how what we think affects how we live. There's a scarcity mindset—believing there is a limited supply of resources, so you grab as much as you can and hoard it. And there's an abundance mindset—believing there is plenty to go around, so you can be generous toward your neighbor.

A scarcity mindset isn't anything new. **Look back at Exodus 16:20. What happened when the Israelites tried to gather more because of this mindset?**

How often have our scarcity mindsets bred worms and become foul in our lives? Where we don't trust in God's abundance? Where we stay tight fisted about our own resources? Where we isolate ourselves from community because of it?

Do you usually trust in God's abundance? Or do you more often subscribe to a scarcity mindset? Why is that? Take a moment to journal your thoughts.

God showed the Israelites His phenomenal provision with quail and manna before He set His commandment about the Sabbath in stone. He was showing them that He would take care of them. Just a few pages later, God gives the Ten Commandments. The commandments are organized into two themes: The first four commands are about honoring God, while the last six commands are about honoring others.

Turn to Exodus 20. Read verses 1-17. Pay special attention to verse 8-11. What stands out to you in that section?

The last thing I want this study to do is lay a new law upon you. We are free from the law; Christ has fulfilled it completely. *The Sabbath is not a requirement; it is a gift.* My great hope is that the ceasing that comes in Sabbath will point us to the manna that may solve our starvation.

We are exhausted.

We are overworked.

We are hurried and busy, anxious and depressed.

We look to our work to find our worth.

This week we will look at what Jesus did with the Sabbath. But for today, I want you to grab onto the gift of ceasing to be God—the gift of stopping. Stop trying to secure your self-worth with accomplishment. Stop hustling for your worth. Stop trying altogether. Instead, start trusting. Enjoy the gift of trusting God to provide. Enjoy the fun of letting God fill your plate. Enjoy the rest that comes when we cease.

Can you recall a time where you were out of energy, resources, finances, or emotional strength, only to see God provide for you? Write about it here.

Now, can you imagine building a rhythm of work and rest into your week? A space to help you stop trying and start trusting that God will take care of you just as He has before? **Journal your thoughts on this.**

THE PRACTICE OF SABBATH

This week, as we continue to prepare to set aside a day to rest, we have to think through what it practically means to trust God on a day we consecrate as holy.

When you think about a Sabbath this week, think about how you can trust God with the areas below.

WORK: (For example, I have to trust God that if I stop writing for one whole day this week, He will provide the time and energy to meet my deadlines. This feels like a big trust fall.)

HOME/FAMILY: (For example, I have to trust God that if I don't get all the laundry done, the bathrooms cleaned, the carpets vacuumed, the pantry re-organized, the refrigerator wiped down, I will be okay. The chores will always be there, so I have to trust that resting means a godly resistance to my personhood being tied to productivity.)

SOCIAL MEDIA: (For example, my work is tied to a social media presence. If I cease social media for a day, I have to trust God that He provides my platform, not me.)

A FULL PLATE OF PEACE

One of my favorite things about studying the Sabbath years ago was uncovering more about what the word itself actually means. I often come back to this thought from Marva Dawn's book *Keeping the Sabbath Wholly*:

> That word, usually rendered "rest," means "much more than withdrawal from labor and exertion, more than freedom from toil, strain or activity of any kind." Rather than a negative concept, the word connotes "something real and intrinsically positive." . . . [The Sabbath is] "tranquility, serenity, peace and repose." . . .
>
> Understanding that Sabbath means peace, we can use the Hebrew word shalom to help us with the idea of rest. Shalom . . . means, most importantly, "peace with God."[1]

When you read the words used to describe Sabbath here—tranquility, serenity, peace, repose, and shalom—what feelings or thoughts come to mind? Which word stands out to you the most?

Resting isn't just the absence of work; it's the presence of peace.

What a gift God wants to give us. He wants us to have a wholeness—a peace that replaces work. He doesn't just want to take our plates away; He wants to fill them with good things.

So, how do we get to a full plate of peace?

We rest in His promises.
We rest in His pasture.
We rest in His provision.

WE REST IN HIS PROMISES.

One of the key elements to help us replace our busyness with God's peace is the Scripture. The Torah was central to observing and remembering the Sabbath. The Israelites turned to it and read stories to remember how God provided for them in the wilderness. They looked to it for reminders of the covenant promises of God. These truths anchored their souls to the real peace and wholeness we receive in God and God alone.

Psalm 23 has been a touchstone for me. In fact, the psalms in general are what I read on Sundays when I Sabbath. What I've learned along the way is this: the practice of remembering God's promises won't make the pain disappear, but it will bring peace in the middle of it.

As we looked at Psalm 23 to start our week, take a moment and slowly read Psalm 23:1-2 in the New Living Translation.

The LORD is my shepherd;
    I have all that I need.
He lets me rest in green meadows;
    he leads me beside peaceful streams.

What promises do you find in these two verses that give you peace?

WE REST IN HIS PASTURE.

We have all that we need. And because we have all that we need, we can rest in green meadows.

Slowly read Psalm 23:1-3 in *The Message*:

> God, my shepherd!
>   I don't need a thing.
> You have bedded me down in lush meadows,
>   you find me quiet pools to drink from.
> True to your word,
>   you let me catch my breath
>   and send me in the right direction.

What speaks to you about resting in the Shepherd's pasture here?

I think of this scene when I nap on Sundays. Whether I close my eyes for ten minutes or two hours, I think of God tucking me in, bedding me down in lush meadows. He is letting me catch my breath and will then send me in the right direction when I wake up.

WE REST IN HIS PROVISION.

Resting and trusting are sisters on the Sabbath. We can't rest if we don't trust that the world will be okay without all of our striving. If we don't believe God is God. If we don't have assurance that God will provide for us while we rest.

Again, read Psalm 23:1-2, this time in the God's Word translation:

> The LORD is my shepherd.
> I am never in need.

He makes me lie down in green pastures.
He leads me beside peaceful waters.

What does the Word say about our need?

This is what Sabbath is all about. It's about resting in all that God gives us. It's about finding nourishment in His promises, His pasture, and His provision. As we plan to Sabbath together this week, my prayer is that you'll find real, deep rest in each of these things.

THE PRACTICE OF SABBATH

This week, as we continue to prepare to set aside a day to rest, take a moment to describe what rest would look like to you. **Consider each area below:**

SPIRITUAL REST:

PHYSICAL REST:

EMOTIONAL REST:

Remember, to Sabbath is an invitation to know God. Use this Scripture as a prayer as you plan to Sabbath this week.

> I am the LORD your God; follow my decrees and be careful to keep my laws. Keep my Sabbaths holy, that they may be a sign between us. Then you will know that I am the LORD your God. **EZEKIEL 20:19-20, NIV**

EMBRACING GOD'S PEOPLE AND PRIORITIES

When I overheard my friend Christy say she had invited ten college students from our church over for Sunday brunch, all I could think was, "Of course she did! Because she loves to embrace people."

Christy is a middle-aged single woman in our church who routinely fills her table with people, food, laughter, and good storytelling. Her second-floor apartment is cozy and inviting. It may not be large, but her heart sure is. And that makes all the difference.

This invitation? This embracing of God's people in her home? This is part of Sabbath for Christy. Maybe it could be for you, too.

See, Sabbath isn't just not doing things. It's not just ceasing and resting. It's also about actions that help you lean into God's Kingdom and priorities. It's about embracing and feasting.

Today is a day to focus on embracing. Specifically, we're going to look at embracing God's people and priorities with intentionality and joy. And of course, Jesus shows us how this is done. Isn't that so like Jesus? Always flipping the script, causing us to remember the heart behind everything God has set up for us.

Read Matthew 12:1-13.

According to verse 7, what does Jesus want people to know the meaning of?

In verse 8, who do we learn is the Lord of the Sabbath?

According to verse 10, what were the Pharisees hoping to do to Jesus? What question do they ask Him?

In verses 11-12, how does Jesus answer them?

God's Kingdom priorities include valuing people over productions. Valuing healing over rules. Valuing mercy over sacrifices. Jesus teaches us that the Sabbath isn't made to rule us; Jesus is. He is the Son of Man, who is Lord of all—including the Sabbath that He set up for us.

Jesus wears His heart on His sleeve when He says, "If any of you has a sheep and it falls into a pit on the Sabbath, will you not take hold of it and lift it out? How much more valuable is a person than a sheep! Therefore it is lawful to do good on the Sabbath" (verses 11-12).

It's almost as if He's saying, "The Sabbath is for more than stopping; it is for embracing good. It is lawful—it is right and beautiful and just—to do good on the Sabbath!"

This brings me back to my friend Christy. That week, her Sabbath included bringing others to the table to feel loved, nourished, and cared for. That's because she values embracing people, sharing her space, being part of rescuing sheep who may have fallen into the pit and may need a soft pasture to land in. It's her calling to open her home and her heart as a means of mercy and compassion. Friend, in making it a priority to embrace these people, she is doing exactly what God desires.

Because we are free in the Spirit, your Sabbath will look very different from anyone else's. It may even look different from week to week. Why? Because this is about listening to God's Spirit and not creating some new law to follow. Some of my Sabbaths have looked full, with people and food, loudness and laughter. Some have looked simpler, with napping and sweats, chips and queso. The goal? Letting God shepherd us and hearing His voice leading us toward what to embrace that day.

Read Jesus' words below.

My sheep hear my voice, and I know them, and they follow me.
JOHN 10:27

What is true about us sheep?

God is our shepherd, and we hear His voice. We know Him, and we follow Him. Let Him lead you as you plan your Sabbath. He wants to feed your starving soul with His goodness. He wants you to embrace the things that matter: His people and His priorities.

THE PRACTICE OF SABBATH

This week, as we continue to prepare to set aside a day to rest, think about what you can embrace. How can you "do good" on the Sabbath?

Write a prayer, asking God what He has for you when it comes to embracing His people and His priorities.

Maybe God is asking you to take a step of faith in regard to fellowship. Could you invite some friends out to lunch? Could you invite a friend on a walk? Could you ask God to show you who around you needs something? What gifts do you have to give on the Sabbath for the good of the Kingdom? What would be fun to do on the Sabbath when it comes to embracing Kingdom values, play, and joy?

Journal your thoughts below.

TIME TO FEAST

I am not sure if you can tell this yet or not, but I love food. I love baking. I love trying new recipes (especially sweet treats). I come from a long line of talented cooks who canned food, made their own ketchup (which is both impressive and tedious), and fed many mouths on tight budgets with food from scratch.

And my favorite thing about food? Sharing it. Sitting at big tables full of family and friends. Passing plates and bumping elbows. Sloshing gravy and telling jokes. It's the best.

When it comes to a weekly Sabbath, delight, joy, and feasting are a big part of this rhythm. In the Israelites' culture, several feasts were set aside during the year to remember God's faithfulness, provision, and goodness. Back then, the Sabbath was seen as a minifeast each week.

Circle the words *delight*, *joy*, and *feast* in the Scripture from Isaiah below.

If you keep your feet from breaking the Sabbath
and from doing as you please on my holy day,
if you call the Sabbath a delight
and the LORD's holy day honorable,
and if you honor it by not going your own way
and not doing as you please or speaking idle words,
then you will find your joy in the LORD,
and I will cause you to ride in triumph on the heights of the land
and to feast on the inheritance of your father Jacob.

ISAIAH 58:13-14, NIV

God loves a good feast. In fact, He's been calling us to His banquet table for quite some time, and He will call us again in the very good ending. Let's look at God's heart.

Read Isaiah 55:1-3. How many times do you see the word "come"?

Turn to John 7:37-39 and read the passage. What is Jesus' invitation to His followers?

Now, read Revelation 22:16-17. What is the call here in the last chapter of the entire Bible? How many times do you see the word "come"?

Many folks today are still waiting on a savior, but we believe Jesus is the Messiah. We are waiting for *His* return. And part of the waiting is practicing what will be the heavenly scene: a banquet table where everything is right. Not one thing is wrong, not one thing is sad, not one thing hurts. This is the table as God intended.

Take a moment to read the sections below from Revelation chapter 19 and 21, underlining anything to do with invitations, weddings, and thirst.

> The angel said to me, "Write this: Blessed are those who are invited to the wedding supper of the Lamb!" And he added, "These are the true words of God."
>
> **REVELATION 19:9, NIV**

Then I saw "a new heaven and a new earth," for the first heaven and the first earth had passed away, and there was no longer any sea. I saw the Holy City, the new Jerusalem, coming down out of heaven from God, prepared as a bride beautifully dressed for her husband. And I heard a loud voice from the throne saying, "Look! God's dwelling place is now among the people, and he will dwell with them. They will be his people, and God himself will be with them and be their God. 'He will wipe every tear from their eyes. There will be no more death' or mourning or crying or pain, for the old order of things has passed away."

He who was seated on the throne said, "I am making everything new!" Then he said, "Write this down, for these words are trustworthy and true."

He said to me: "It is done. I am the Alpha and the Omega, the Beginning and the End. To the thirsty I will give water without cost from the spring of the water of life. Those who are victorious will inherit all this, and I will be their God and they will be my children."

REVELATION 21:1-7, NIV

Speaking of a supper, what did Jesus instruct us to do to remember Him? (see 1 Corinthians 11:23-26)

Jesus instructed us to remember Him with a meal—a feast. The night before He died, He gave us bread and wine, to remember His body and blood.[1] One of the things I like about taking a Sabbath day on Sunday is we take communion as part of our feasting at church. We remember what Jesus did so we can be invited to His table. It is a time to fellowship with one another, to worship, to commune, to remember the table and all that it means.

Just in case you are second-guessing whether you are invited to the feast, read the last line of Revelation 21:7. What are the victorious called?

Some have said feasting is meaningful only when we've experienced the other side. Feasting is elevated when we've also known fasting. Marva Dawn writes about how she often keeps to very simple meals during the week to look forward to rich foods on the Sabbath. She likes to stick to oatmeal all week to enjoy a more elaborate breakfast on her day of rest. The role of simplicity during her week ushers in the rich delight of the Sabbath. I love that idea. I think I might practice for a week and see how that goes.

> Yet to all who did receive him, to those who believed in his name, he gave the right to become children of God—children born not of natural descent, nor of human decision or a husband's will, but born of God.
> **JOHN 1:12-13, NIV**

As promised, you will have everything you need to be able to Sabbath by the end of this week's study. We talked through ceasing, resting, embracing, and feasting. We looked at the gift of the Sabbath rather than the burden of it. We looked at trusting God to be God on the Sabbath. And we talked about preparing to Sabbath. Now, friend, is the time to step into the Sabbath together.

As you think about taking a day to Sabbath, what are your thoughts now?

THE PRACTICE OF SABBATH

This week, we have been journaling thoughts on a whole day of rest. Take a moment to look back over this week and the thoughts you journaled at the end of each day.

What preparations do you need to make?

What are you looking forward to?

If you have a family, have you talked with them about what the Sabbath could look like?

I'll leave you with this thought from author Eugene Peterson that has encouraged me in this practice:

> If we do not regularly quit work for one day a week, we take ourselves far too seriously. The moral sweat pouring off our brows blinds our eyes to the action of God in and around us.[2]

AMY'S HONEY LEMONADE

This is one of my family's all-time favorites. Why? Because everyone loves to squeeze lemons in my house . . . to the point of fighting over who gets to juice the most. All that to say, making this lemonade is a perfect summer activity that turns into a treat! It's also a lovely Sunday-afternoon drink (our Sabbath) to relax with on the back patio.

Ingredients

1 cup lemon juice (freshly squeezed is best—about 1 lb. lemons)

½–¾ cup raw honey (if you like your lemonade sweeter, you can add a little more)

3 cups water

1–2 cups ice cubes

Instructions

1. Squeeze lemons or measure out lemon juice.
2. Add honey to water in a large saucepan to make a simple syrup. Heat until honey is absorbed into the water. Remove from heat.
3. After placing ice in pitcher, add fresh-squeezed lemon juice on top. Then pour the honey syrup over the lemon juice.
4. Mix and enjoy! To sweeten further, add another squeeze of honey.

STARVED FOR JUSTICE

Questions for Discussion

THE PROBLEM
What is starving us in our pursuit of justice?

THE PROMISE
What Scriptures have been feeding your soul lately?

THE PRACTICE
What spiritual practice can satiate you when your soul is starved for justice?

PERSONAL REFLECTION
Choose a question and take a moment to journal.

- What is your view of God and justice? How has it changed over time?
- If justice (*mishpat*) also includes proactive care for the marginalized, how might you be able practice justice in your own life?
- Who is marginalized in your neighborhood, community, church, or city? What resources do you have to share?

Video sessions available for download at amyseiffert.com.

STARVED FOR JUSTICE

To get the most out of this week's study, read chapter 5 of *Starved*.

MORE THAN WORDS

You've seen it on cute little plaques and lovely wooden signs. You might even have one hanging up right now in your hallway.

I do.

In my home, it's a beautiful metal sign made by none other than Jimmy Don from Chip and Jo's Magnolia Market. It was a gift, and I adore it. It reads:

Act justly, love mercy, walk humbly.

Maybe these six words are familiar to you. Maybe they're more than familiar. Maybe they're important, powerful, aspirational in your mind. When I see those words hanging in my home, they make me feel good, well-meaning.

They're words the prophet Micah said. Words we can find in the Old Testament in the book titled with his name. And, yes, while they sound great and even look great on home decor, when I really think about it, there's more to these words than we might initially realize.

What do they actually mean?

Why did the prophet say them?

Why do we give them to one another as gifts?

Why are they on mugs or artwork?

This week, we will talk about these words. We'll look at justice, mercy, and humility together. And as we do, we'll discover that these are so much more than words.

They're a call to live our lives in pursuit of what's good, holy, and right.

They're a call to the work of justice.

If you're anything like me, the idea of justice has felt a bit mysterious and abstract at times. I wasn't explicitly taught about justice in the church. I don't ever remember hearing one sermon on it. For most of my life, I had no idea what justice meant in the Kingdom of God. I don't even think I understood it in its biblical context until I was forty (which is not that long ago).

But in the summer of 2020, that all changed.

Likely because the world changed. Or maybe the world—or at least the white part of the world—just finally woke up. I know I did.

COVID-19 ravaged our world. Then, specifically in our country, communities of color were harmed by more than just the virus. On shaky phone videos and blurry dashboard cameras, we saw Black men and women harassed, wounded, and even killed. Story after story hit the news of Asian Americans being targeted in random attacks. Suddenly, the things we knew were there—the racism, the prejudice, the bias, the pain—were right in front of our faces.

And friends, we can't look away.

That summer, it was clear to me in a new way: we are starving for justice. We have been for a long time. And we have to do something about it.

As people who have Bible verses about justice plastered on metal signs in our homes.

As believers in the God who made us all in His image.

As followers of Jesus.

We have to learn what it really means to do what God called us to do.

Act justly, love mercy, walk humbly.

That summer, those became more than words for so many of us. Almost overnight, white evangelical churches started talking about justice. Thankfully, they got the same wake-up call. They saw the need to step into the holy work of justice in this world.

But before I could step into that work that so many of our brothers and sisters in Christ have been doing for so long, I needed to do some of my own work. I needed to dive into my own heart and soul. I needed to understand how justice fits into the Kingdom of God.

That's exactly what I hope we'll do together this week. Let's wade into this verse slowly and with grace. I imagine this week's journey like entering a pool. We will start in shallow waters and make our way deeper. But I promise, your feet will always be on the ground.

And where we discover ourselves to be starved, my prayer is that we'll find that justice nourishes.

WHAT IS GOOD . . .

The year I turned forty, some things turned upside down in my life.

What were these new back pains?

Why didn't my muscles recover as fast after workouts?

Why were things achy and creaky? Slouchy and saggy?

Add in a worldwide pandemic that year, and well, I was a bundle of fun.

The world shut down just a few days before I was set to go on a trip of a lifetime to Israel for ten days. You better believe I cried into my chips and queso for days. This was also just a few weeks before the release of my first devotional, *Grace Looks Amazing on You*, so the book signings, the speaking events, and all the related fun had to be canceled.

I was discouraged, disappointed, and certainly down and out about it all. When the calendar flipped to my fortieth year, nothing—not one thing—turned out the way I thought it would.

Maybe you can relate. I'd venture to say the early days of 2020 left us all more than a little shaken up. And by the time summer came? Well, then it seemed the world flipped upside down completely.

The names and faces of brothers and sisters made in the image of God—brothers and sisters who don't look like me—hit the news almost daily. Brothers and sisters who were victimized simply because of the color of their skin. Brothers and sisters who needed us to stand up for justice.

As protest after protest materialized across the entire globe, I saw the signs and the shouts for justice. I saw the names. I heard the cries. I watched the footage. I recognized the deep starvation for God's good and right justice in each one.

With each story that unfolded, it felt as if a thirty-pound brick was dropped inside of my stomach. Salty tears soaked my pillow.

Why, Lord?

Why such violence?

Why such oppression?

Why such injustice?

That summer, the sign I walked past a dozen times suddenly stopped me.

Write out Micah 6:8 below.

Let's talk about the first part of this verse: "He has told you, mortal one, what is good; and what does the Lord require of you?" (NASB 1995).

The book of Micah is a short but powerful prophecy. It predicts the fall of Jerusalem and Samaria and offers hope that a "remnant of Jacob" will later be restored (see Micah 5:7). In chapter 6, God uses Micah to remind His people of how He has cared for them in the past. Micah questions how in the world the people could be restored to God. He wonders what it will take. In other words, what will it require of them?

Turn to Micah 6:7. What does the prophet think it might take to be restored to God?

Turns out, it isn't a sacrifice God wants.

Micah reminds himself that God has already shown the way. Years before, after God rescued the Israelites from slavery and they crossed the Red Sea, He gave them the way to life.

Let's recall what God said here. Read Deuteronomy 6:1-12. Write out verses 4-6.

Where does God say these commands should live, according to verse 6?

God wants our hearts. He wants a heart that loves. He showed this to the Israelites long before Micah. And now, Micah remembers it. Loving God and others—that's what God requires of us. That is what's good. And, as Micah puts it, that looks like acting justly, loving mercy, and walking humbly.

> God's heart—His desire—for us is to act justly, love mercy, walk humbly.

That question in verse 8 is important to understand: "What does the LORD require of you?" The idea of "require" here has nothing to do with our salvation. That's already been sealed and done with on the Cross. The idea is living out our faith in light of His grace. This isn't a demand; it's what God's heart wants for us.

God's heart—His desire—for us is to act justly, love mercy, walk humbly.

And it's a desire that's good. A desire that will nourish a world starving for justice.

What I love about this verse is that it connects our heart with our hands. Our faith with our actions. There are three verbs attached to this call of what God desires of us—of what it means to love the Lord God with all of who we are. This week, we will look at each one.

But for today, let's stop here. Let's close by looking at how Jesus summed up in His own words what God requires of us. In the book of Matthew, a teacher asks Jesus a very straightforward question. And Jesus gives a straightforward answer.

"Teacher, which is the greatest commandment in the Law?"

Jesus replied: "'Love the Lord your God with all your heart and with all your soul and with all your mind.' This is the first and greatest commandment. And the second is like it: 'Love your neighbor as yourself.' All the Law and the Prophets hang on these two commandments."

MATTHEW 22:36-40, NIV

Sounds familiar right? *God has not changed.* Love is the call from Moses to the Messiah. Love God and love your neighbor. Micah is just getting specific about what it looks like to enjoy a restored life with God.

And friend, that is what is good.

> **God has not changed. Love is the call from Moses to the Messiah.**

THE PRACTICE OF JUSTICE

Together, let's consider what is good—what God desires for us. The call to love God and love others with all we've got. **How would you connect justice work to loving your neighbor? Journal your thoughts here.**

To close, take a moment to pray:

God, thank You that You have shown us the way. Thank You that Jesus became the living way of life. Teach me to do what is good. To do what You desire of me. Help me to have a heart to love others the way You do. Help me to love You and love those made in Your image well.

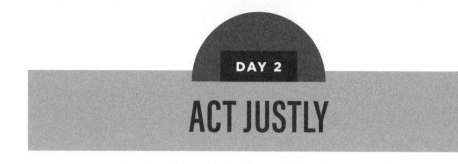

ACT JUSTLY

Act justly.

This is the first thing Micah lays out for us. When we're considering what it means to love God with our whole selves, the first call is this: to act justly. Some translations say "do justice" here. And in a world starving for justice, this feels like a good place to start.

So, what does that mean? Let's start by thinking about justice.

The World Vision website defines it this way:

Biblical references to the word "justice" mean "to make right."
Justice is, first and foremost, a relational term—people living in right relationship with God, one another, and the natural creation. From a scriptural point of view, justice means loving our neighbor as we love ourselves and is rooted in the character and nature of God. As God is just and loving, so we are called to do justice and live in love.[1]

Think about the life of Jesus and this definition of justice—to make right. How did Jesus do this in His life and ministry? Write down as many ways as you can in which Jesus made things right.

If justice means making things right, then that's exactly what Jesus came to do.

He made the blind see.

He made the lame walk.

He made the outcast in.

He took the least of these and called them the greatest.

He gave women back their dignity.

Jesus came to make things right in every single kind of way—socially, spiritually, and everything in between. The ultimate act of justice? The Cross. The curtain was torn from top to bottom in the Temple so we could have a right relationship with God again. There, things were made right.

God's heart has always been for the vulnerable, the oppressed, the outcast, the marginalized. God's heart has always been for us to be nourished with what's good. God's heart has always been for justice.

The more I meditated on what it means to make things right, the more I had to be honest with myself about why justice hasn't always been on my radar. I have never had to cry out for justice in ways my protesting friends have for centuries. The scales have tipped my way. I have not been wronged in ways that cause me to grasp at justice. I have been insulated and isolated from injustice.

The more I started to search the Scriptures for justice in an attempt to understand a God who is just, the more I couldn't believe I had missed it all along. It's like the moment I found out I was pregnant. All of a sudden, I saw pregnant women everywhere. My eyes were opened, and I couldn't unsee them. That's because whatever you focus on is what your eyes will see.

I hadn't been focused on this call for justice, and because of that, I missed the foundational truth about who God is and what His entire throne has been built upon.

Read Isaiah 9:6-7. Who will establish God's Kingdom? What will He uphold that Kingdom with?

Read Psalm 89:14. What is the foundation of God's throne?

Read Amos 5:24. What does Amos want to roll like waters?

Read Matthew 23:23-24. What does Jesus say are the important matters of the law?

Read Isaiah 1:17. What five things does God want us to learn?

Can we stop and celebrate here? Friend, we have a God who knows we need to learn. We are fumbling, uncovering, changing, growing, and in need of the grace to learn and do better. And God knows that. He has grace ready for it.

He calls us to keep learning.

Keep growing.

Keep changing.

Keep doing better.

Keep growing into the image of His Son.

He calls us to act justly and gives us the grace we need to do just that.

THE PRACTICE OF JUSTICE

This week, consider the definition of justice—making things right. Think through the spiritual, physical, emotional, and relational aspects of your life. How has God made things right in your life? **Journal some thoughts below.**

To close, take a moment to pray:

God, You are so good and kind and compassionate. Your throne is built upon making things right and giving the vulnerable their rights. How glorious of You! You are a father to the fatherless and a defender of the widow. Enlarge my heart to see, and feel, and have compassion on those who are in need. Show me how You want me to "do justice" in light of who You are. Lead me. I am listening.

LOVE MERCY

Poor people are just lazy.

If they would just stop doing drugs and get their act together. . . .

They are just taking advantage of the system. I'm not letting them take advantage of me.

You've probably heard things like this before. Maybe your grandfather said these things at holidays. Maybe you've heard them from a neighbor. Maybe you think these thoughts, even if you've never said them out loud. Or maybe you have.

Either way, it just got real in here. It has to get real in here.

Today, we are looking at Micah's call to love mercy, but in order to do that, we've got to be honest with ourselves. If we want to progress from starving to satisfied, we've got to be real about where we're starting.

As we jump in today, let's remember our verse for the week.

Write down Micah 6:8 again here.

God wants us to "love mercy," or in some translations, "kindness." This is the Hebrew word *hesed*, which can be used to refer to God's loving-kindness to us. God wants us to be drawn to mercy—having kindness and compassion for those in need. And this is directly related to justice. It is out of a deep mercy and loving-kindness that we would make things right.

I think one of the biggest deterrents to our ability to be merciful to others is forgetting how merciful God has been to us. I've heard it said that mercy is not getting what you deserve, and grace is getting what you don't deserve. Thanks be to God that He gives us both.

> It is out of a deep mercy and loving-kindness that we would make things right.

Take a minute and consider how you have NOT gotten what you deserve in your life. Journal a few thoughts here.

To help us dive deeper here, let's take a look at mercy according to the following passages.

Read Luke 6:36-37. Write out verse 36 below. Underline who was merciful to you.

Now, read Lamentations 3:22-23. What is new each morning?

Finally, read Matthew 5:7. Who will be shown mercy?

Some of us have hearts easily bent toward mercy, and some of us (me!) have to learn mercy. I know it's easy to harden our hearts and judge others. It's easy to stay far away from those who aren't like us or who we don't understand. It's easy to make people into flat, small characters. It's easy to not get close. It's easy to refuse to see the complex, multidimensional, made-in-the-image-of-God human beings around us. It's easy to stay free from the mess of it all.

One way I learned to love mercy was through an organization called the Open Table.[1] It's a grassroots model designed to help you use your social capital—all the relationships you have that give you access to resources—to come alongside the needs of those who are financially, relationally, or emotionally poor. Before I served with them, I admit that I thought many of those thoughts (and more I don't even want to admit) mentioned at the start of this day's study. But after? Well, things changed. Mercy changed me.

And because of it, I learned three things:

1. Being trusted and trusting others is a sacred practice.

What a gift it is to be slowly trusted, more and more, with someone's story. With their heartache. With their joy. With their absurdity. With their grace. With their laughter. What a gift to entrust your story to them in the same way. We all come from such different worlds, but we are letting each other in. And it's good. It's nourishing. It's mercy at work.

Have you ever been trusted with someone else's story and had it change you? Or have you trusted someone else with your story in a way that impacted you? Write about it here.

2. Climbing out of poverty is complicated.

Systems are really broken. Poverty is incredibly complex. Nothing is simple. Legislation can't heal hearts, but human connection can. Social capital is a powerful thing—a beautiful gift so many have to give.

What's one way you can use your social capital to help someone who needs it in your community, church, school, or even the world?

3. Compassion only happens when you're up close and personal.

I love that this work puts me in shoes I've never had. And vice versa. Compassion erases shame, and I think our world could use a big, huge dose of that about now. Maybe several doses. Let's just all overdose on compassion, empathy, mercy, and grace. Let's commit to doing that by getting up close and personal with one another.

What is one social issue you struggle to understand? What's one way you can take a step toward getting up close and personal and learning more about what you've struggled to empathize with?

God is calling us to an up-close-and-personal compassion that lets our hearts break for those in need. He desires that we love mercy, because He loves mercy. He desires that we remember the mercy upon us, so that we can be merciful upon others. He blesses the merciful, because they will be shown mercy. He knows that in showing mercy to one another, we'll begin to ease the starvation that's permeating our world.

THE PRACTICE OF JUSTICE

Today, let's reflect on mercy. **How does God's mercy speak to you? How does it challenge you?**

To close, take a moment to pray:

God, I praise You for Your endless mercy. Forgive me for not showing mercy. Show me how to love mercy. Help me to have a heart for kindness and compassion toward others, and use that heart to spur me on to action that supports Your heart for justice.

WALK HUMBLY

Today, by and large, we use cars, planes, and trains to get where we need to in life. Of course, I do love a good bicycle, but only when it's warm out. Bikes are less fun in the snow.

But before all these advances came our way, walking was the primary mode of transportation. In fact, the concept of walking was a common metaphor used in Scripture to talk about not only getting from here to there but about the entire way of life you are choosing. Walking means the direction you are going. It's about the path you're on. You'll see the idea of walking all over God's Word.

With many teachers and rabbis, following in their actual footsteps was a way to learn from them. It was a way to walk around with them and learn their way of life up close. When Jesus called His disciples, He put it this way: "Follow me, and I will make you fishers of men" (Matthew 4:19).

Jesus was calling the disciples to drop their nets, change their jobs, and follow His footsteps. He was calling them to His way of life. To walk with Him. And you know what? They did. With their actual feet, they got up and walked with Jesus.

This is so important for us today. Because the invitation is the same for us. Jesus has called us to walk in His ways, and friend, our walk is our way of life.

What I appreciate about Micah is that he was a practical man. He didn't just tell us to walk, he wanted us to know how to walk. So, he added the adverb "humbly" to tell us how.

In your own words, how would you describe humility?

Here is one of the best definitions I've seen of humility: "This is true humility: not thinking less of ourselves but thinking of ourselves *less*."[1]

Merriam-Webster's dictionary tells us that humility is "freedom from pride or arrogance."[2] In other words, not thinking you are better than other people.

But to help us understand how humility helps us end our starvation for justice, let's look at what the Bible says.

Read 2 Chronicles 7:14. When will God hear, forgive, and heal the Israelites' land?

Now look at Proverbs 11:2. What comes with wisdom?

Turn to read Romans 12:16. Who are we supposed to associate with?

Read Colossians 3:12. What are we to clothe ourselves with?

Finally, look up Philippians 2:3. How are we to value others?

Word-nerd alert. I am particularly struck by the verbs in this last verse. So, we are going to slow down and read the fuller context in the second chapter of Philippians and pay attention to the verbs. **Read the entirety of this passage below. As you do, underline the verbs.**

> Do nothing out of selfish ambition or vain conceit. Rather, in humility value others above yourselves, not looking to your own interests but each of you to the interests of the others.
>
> In your relationships with one another, have the same mindset as Christ Jesus:
>
> Who, being in very nature God,
> did not consider equality with God something to be used to his own
> advantage;
> rather, he made himself nothing
> by taking the very nature of a servant,
> being made in human likeness.
> And being found in appearance as a man,
> he humbled himself
> by becoming obedient to death—
> even death on a cross!
>
> Therefore God exalted him to the highest place
> and gave him the name that is above every name,
> that at the name of Jesus every knee should bow,
> in heaven and on earth and under the earth,
> and every tongue acknowledge that Jesus Christ is Lord,
> to the glory of God the Father.

PHILIPPIANS 2:3-11, NIV

Look at the verbs—the action words—you underlined. Which one stands out to you the most?

Here's what I love about the verbs in this passage: God is not calling us to do anything His Son has not done before us. He is calling us to walk with Him, and in Jesus He has shown us how. When we put our feet to pavement to walk with God, we are following in the footsteps of His Son.

We are following in the way that acts justly, loves mercy, and walks humbly.

We are following the path to justice.

THE PRACTICE OF JUSTICE

Today we focused on what it means to walk humbly with God. What did you learn about walking humbly? How does this relate to the work of justice?

To close this week, we will build toward an action step with justice work, but before we could do that, we've had to take our time to listen and learn God's heart for justice. Today, let's open our hands in humility.

To close, take a moment to pray:

Father, I come humbly before You. I want to walk in humility. Show me how to value others above myself. Show me how to think less of myself and more of others and their needs. Specifically, give me a humble heart to love, support, and defend the marginalized, the distressed, the orphan, the widow, the oppressed. Lead me and guide me as I walk with You in this work. Amen.

IMAGO DEI

We have taken our time considering Micah 6:8 this week. I mean, we spent four days on one verse! You may very well have it memorized by now (which is awesome!). I am sure you are beginning to see how starved our world is for justice. I'm sure you've seen how much God desires to use us to help make things right.

One more time, write Micah 6:8 below.

Micah's call to all of humanity is God's desire for us to act justly, love mercy, and walk humbly. But friends, when we have failed to do this (and we all have), we have failed to honor the dignity inside every single human being. The dignity given to us on the first page of the Bible. The dignity that is ours as those made in the image of our God.

Write out Genesis 1:27 below.

We were formed in the image of God. The Latin phrase used for this is *imago Dei*, meaning we reflect the nature of God Himself. We are unique and set apart from any other creature. Created with dignity, value, and worth, we are people made in God's own majestic likeness.

127

One of the deepest implications of being made in God's image is that we are made to love. We are to love God and to love one another. Because not only are we made in God's image—and God is love—but our image-bearing dignity demands the respect, honor, and care we'd give to anyone we love. Anyone made in God's image. Anyone God has called us to love as His own.

Who does this apply to? Anyone on Earth, because anyone and everyone is made in the image of our God. Our very significance is stamped on our souls. We are imago Dei, the image of God. We ought to honor this in ourselves and honor it in others.

Remember, the call to act justly means we are called to make things right. The Hebrew word for justice is *mishpat*, and it is mentioned over two hundred times in the Bible. Ninety percent of the time, the word was used to describe proactive care and giving people their rights.[1]

That is justice work. That is nourishing work. That is the work of defending, supporting, and loving the imago Dei in everyone, but especially in the marginalized.

So, let's consider where we see God demonstrate proactive care for the marginalized, poor, and oppressed. Anyone who has been shoved to the edge of society. Anyone who hasn't been treated as if they bear the very image of God on their souls.

Read Leviticus 23:22. Who are the Israelites to leave the edges of the field for?

Turn to read Deuteronomy 27:19. Who is cursed?

Read Psalm 68:4-5. How does God describe Himself here?

Now, look up Zechariah 7:10-11. Who are we not to oppress?

What does Proverbs 31:8 tell us to do?

And of course, we have the four Gospels that detail the life of Jesus and His humble walk. He was constantly moving toward, repairing, and restoring those on the margins of society. Those who had less social capital, financial stability, and respect, fewer resources and rights. Those who needed others to use their voices on their behalf. Those who were starving for justice.

Jesus loved children.

And women.

And the sick.

And the lame.

And the blind.

And the lepers.

And the rejected rich, like Zacchaeus.

And the hated ethnicities, like Samaritans.

And the poor.

And the disenfranchised.

Jesus loved those the world didn't always. Jesus not only saw the imago Dei in them, but He spoke up for it. He defended it. He fought for it. And friend, as followers of Jesus, we are called to do the same.

To sum it up, who did Jesus say He came for according to Mark 2:16-17?

Jesus restored the dignity that was denied to so many. Jesus was a man of justice. And if we want to stop the starvation, the oppression, the hatred, the pain, the inequality, and more in our world, we have to be people of justice in the same way.

Justice says, "I see my dignity, value, and worth, and I also see yours. I honor the imago Dei inside of me. And I honor it inside of you. I protect the imago Dei in you. I will fight for the imago Dei in you. I will treat the imago Dei in you with love, compassion, and care."

Justice is calling us (especially those of us in the majority) to take action. My prayer for us as we close this week is that we'll boldly and bravely answer that call.

That we will pursue justice for the sake of God's Kingdom and the imago Dei in us all.

As we consider our journey through justice this week, let's close by looking to ourselves. This isn't easy, friend, but remember, there is grace here for all of us. So, let's commit to being honest with ourselves.

Where have you denied dignity to others in your heart or your actions? Where have you seen others as less-than? Where have you failed to see, acknowledge, or defend the imago Dei in others?

Close by writing an honest prayer to God, asking Him to forgive where you've failed and spur you on to listen, learn, and love others as made in His image.

THE PRACTICE OF JUSTICE

As we close this week, consider all the resources God has given you: time, money, energy, skills, the place you live, a car, your food, your personality, and more.

With those things in mind, ask God to show you how He wants you to take action.

Is it serving at a food pantry? Is it visiting those who are incarcerated? Is it finding social justice organizations and supporting them? Is it inviting your neighbor who is a widow for dinner or taking her food? Is it researching organizations doing justice work in your community and considering joining? Is it listening, learning, and lamenting American history, and then leveraging your privilege to lift up folks who have been marginalized by it? We studied a list of verbs this week, so think in terms of actions.

Write your thoughts below.

Consider this prayer from author and activist Latasha Morrison:

> Lord, we confess as a church that we have modified the meaning of the gospel to justify our lack of effort to pursue justice for the oppressed. We have altered the nature of the gospel message in order to remain focused on our personal piety at the expense of caring for the needs of others. We confess we have created a gospel that is manageable so as to avoid entering into the pain, struggle, and discomfort of bearing one another's burdens—and therefore we have failed to fulfill the law of Christ.[2]

To close, take a moment to pray:

> *God, I am made in Your image. Help me to recognize this in myself. Then, help me to see that same beautiful, diverse image in others. Forgive me for how I've failed to do that in the past. Now, lead me in not just seeing and loving the image of You in others, but in defending, supporting, and fighting for it as well. This is the nourishing work of justice our world is starving for, and I want to be part of it with You. So, give me ears to listen, a heart to understand, and courage to step into this important work in Your Kingdom. Amen.*

PESTO PASTA AND GARLIC BUTTER SHRIMP

Some of my favorite conversations about justice work have happened around good food with our friends in the organization BRAVE (bravebg.org). Laughing, sharing, playing, learning, eating together—it's been such a gift. And somehow it always ends in a fierce game of basketball knockout in the driveway, which I love (and have won, mind you). This is one of our go-to dishes, which feels like a fancy treat but is so easy. I usually keep a box of pasta, a jar of pesto, and frozen shrimp on hand, just in case. Fancy and easy? I'm in.

Ingredients

1 box of your favorite pasta (we love cauliflower lentil pasta by Veggiecraft Farms)

1 stick butter

2-3 tbsp. minced garlic

1-2 lbs. thawed shrimp (deveined, frozen, tail off)

salt and pepper, to taste

1 jar of your favorite pesto (we love DeLallo—olive oil, basil, cashew nuts, and parmesan)

Instructions

1. Cook pasta in a large saucepan according to package directions.

2. While pasta is cooking, heat a large frying pan with butter and garlic until butter is melted and you smell the garlic cooking.

3. Add shrimp and season with salt and pepper. Sauté until pink and opaque. Set aside.

4. Once pasta is cooked, drain it in a colander and return the pasta to the pan. Add 5-6 tablespoons pesto until the pasta is covered. Toss until coated.

5. To serve, put a generous amount of pasta on a plate or in a pasta bowl, and top with shrimp. *Wham!* You are a hero.

STARVED FOR IDENTITY

Questions for Discussion

THE PROBLEM
What is starving us in our search for identity?

THE PROMISE
What Scriptures have been feeding your soul lately?

THE PRACTICE
What spiritual practice can satiate you when your soul is starved for your true identity?

PERSONAL REFLECTION
Choose a question and take a moment to journal.

- What has worked for you in the past when it comes to knowing your identity in Christ?
- How has prayer helped you in knowing your identity?
- What happens in your life when you make others' voices higher than God's voice?

Video sessions available for download at amyseiffert.com.

STARVED FOR IDENTITY

To get the most out of this week's study, read chapter 9 of *Starved*.

LISTEN TO GOD FIRST

Change can be the worst, right?

If you have ever moved, or started a new job, or stepped into a new church where no one knows who you are, or what you love, or what you are good at, you have felt it. You know what I mean. Change has a way of causing us to question everything we've known about who we are.

Just like that, you are starved for identity. For being known. For being seen. For being loved.

It seems I run into an identity crisis about once every five to seven years. Because that's about the time when friendships shift, jobs change, moves happen. This is when I start thinking all kinds of thoughts about myself.

What am I even doing with my life?

Who am I?

What do people see?

Is my inner life congruent with my outer life?

Have you been there? Are you there now? Thirsting to know who you are? Starving to discover what you're really about?

Some of the wrestling can come from what people have said you are.

A drama queen.

A funny girl.

A responsible woman.

And while some of those labels have made you proud, others have likely brought you pain. I know that's been the case for me.

There are certain labels that have been slapped on me that I didn't ask for and have had trouble reckoning with. As I try to peel them off, like a name tag that's been washed on a shirt and left a stubborn residue, I can't quite seem to get away from them.

I have been told I am irresponsible by some, and by others, extremely responsible.

I have been told I am stupid by some, and by others, smart.

I have been told I am not enough by some, and by others, too much.

So, which is it? Who am I really? Whose voice can I trust to speak life over my starving need to grasp an identity?

I wish someone had sat me down early in my life and said what I heard from a panel of wise women just a few years ago. They were discussing the idea of calling, discovering who God made us to be and the gifts we have been given. Finally, one of the panelists said:

"Listen to God first."

Those four words changed everything for me. When it comes to most things in life, this advice stands. But specifically as it relates to identity, I think there's so much power in these four little words.

Listen to God first.

If God has laid it on your heart to speak or write or teach or encourage or lead or serve, listen to Him first. If God has called you to step out and take a chance, listen to Him first. If God has called you to speak up or show up, listen to Him first.

I think about Mary Magdalene as she went to anoint Jesus' body after His death. There, she ended up running right into the resurrected Lord. He told her not to cling to Him but to go and find the disciples and tell them He was risen. And so, she went. She ran. She obeyed. And from there? The world began to believe.

Because she *listened to God first.*

Pretty amazing, right? Well, let's picture the story differently. What if instead of just going, she stopped by a friend's house to see what she thought of her doing this? What if she second-guessed what she was told to do? What if she went to others to see if it was okay for her to be doing this?

Been there.

Truth be told, we all struggle to listen first and only to God's voice in our lives. But friend, that's what keeps us questioning, doubting, and starving for identity in Him.

So, this week, as we so often starve for identity, let's find ourselves coming to God, first. How do we do that? What does this mean? Let's dive in.

HOW DOES GOD SPEAK?

In my early years of being a follower of Jesus, some people told me they "felt like God was speaking" to them. Some examples were the urge to share the Good News of Jesus with a friend, the call to do something really generous, or even the leading on what college to attend.

To be honest, I wasn't sure what they meant at the time. Was God audibly speaking to them? Did I miss the memo? What does listening to God even look like?

The more I read in the Scriptures, the more I saw that God speaks to people in a variety of ways. In the very beginning, He spoke and the world was created. Later He spoke directly to people through a burning bush, through a pillar of smoke, through a cloud, through wind, through a donkey. And that's just to name a few.

Read Hebrews 1:1-3 below.

In the past God spoke to our ancestors through the prophets at many times and in various ways, but in these last days he has spoken to us by his Son, whom he appointed heir of all things, and through whom also he made the universe. The Son is the radiance of God's glory and the exact representation of his being, sustaining all things by his powerful word. After he had provided purification for sins, he sat down at the right hand of the Majesty in heaven.
HEBREWS 1:1-3, NIV

How did God speak in the past and how, according to the writer of Hebrews, has God spoken in the last days?

God has spoken to the prophets many times, in various ways! And what a gift we have in the written accounts of the life of Jesus! He spoke by living His life and by teaching us.

For you, what does listening to God look like?

Of the list below, circle any of the ways you have heard from God in the past.

His Word   Community

Prayer   The Holy Spirit

Songs   Dreams

Nature   Other: _____

Visions   _____

I have never heard an audible voice from God, but I have heard from Him in a variety of ways. I have read His Word and felt like God was coming through the pages and into my heart. I have had an image, a person, or an idea that lines right up with God's character or His calling to me come to mind in prayer. I have experienced God speaking to me through others and their encouragement. When it aligns with Scripture, I know I can trust it.

But for all the ways I've heard and experienced God's voice in my life, I still find myself tempted to listen to the voices, opinions, and thoughts of others before Him.

Why do you think we sometimes tend to listen to others more than God?

What might happen if we always listened to God first?

I think the answer here depends on what others say to us. Are they telling us lies? Half-truths? Are they bringing us encouragement about the gifts we have? Or are they trying to drag us down so they can feel powerful? Are their words lining up with God's words?

This is where the practice of prayer soothes our parched souls. It helps us parse out what is for us and what isn't. It helps us find nourishment in the right voices and disregard the ones that may contribute to our starvation. I routinely take the words of others to God in prayer. I ask things like this:

Is this what I ought to be doing?
Is this what You are asking of me? Or is it a human request?
What part of this is for me? And what do I need to let go of?
Who do You say I am? Does this line up with that identity?

When we let the voices of others speak over our identity, we have to hold their words up to what is true about who we are. So today, let's go back there—to a verse that reminds us what Jesus says about us.

Read John 10:27-30. What is true of Jesus' sheep according to these verses? Write as many things as you can find.

God has given you the ability to hear Him in a way that is unique to YOU. You may not hear Him like your friend does, or your pastor does, or that Christian author does. But He does speak to you. He wants to speak to you. We just have to tune our ears to hear Him.

One of the ways God speaks consistently to me is through His Word. In fact, these verses from John have been particularly meaningful to me as I listen for His voice.

Turn to Ephesians 4:11-12 (NLT). Fill in the blanks with the five different gifts Paul says were given to the church.

"These are the gifts Christ gave to the church: the _____, the _____, the _____, and the _____ and _____. Their responsibility is to equip God's people to do his work and build up the church, the body of Christ."

What was most clear to me was how not one single gender was assigned to the five gifts listed. They are given to the church, and in case you need a refresher, the church is made up of both men and women. Both are gifted to be apostles, prophets, evangelists, pastors (shepherds), and teachers.

God spoke to me when I read this verse. I had long felt called to teach and pastor, but as a woman, not every circle I sat in affirmed this calling. But in God's Word, the calling I had felt so deep down in my soul to teach and pastor was affirmed. I was starving for it, and I found my nourishment in God's Word.

Is there something you feel called to do but you aren't confident in? Why is that?

What negative words from others have become a soundtrack for your mind, keeping you from trying to live out something God is calling you to do?

Using your Bible's concordance, a Bible app, or even an Internet search, look up a verse that speaks directly to what you feel God has called you to. Write that verse below to help you listen to God's voice first!

THE PRACTICE OF PRAYER

This week, we will engage in five different prayer practices. There are so many ways to pray! Remember, God can speak through a cloud, a burning bush, a dream, a quiet whisper, His Word—anything! And we can use our bodies and our minds to participate in hearing God speak to our identity.

Today's practice is to pray with one other person, something called corporate prayer. This might be a big risk for you if you have never done this before. But one of my favorite things to do is to reach out to a friend and pray with her for a minute or two. You don't have to be in the room together if that's not comfortable for you. You can call. If you have never done this, blame me. You can literally say, "This Amy Seiffert girl is making me do this." I'll take the heat.

Just yesterday I called a friend and said, "Girl, I need prayer. . . . " And I shared that I ran into an old narrative about being flaky and disorganized. I wanted God to rewrite that story, and I needed her prayers to help me. So, she prayed for me, right there on the phone. Then I asked how I could pray for her. She paused before sharing her own requests, and we prayed together over her. I will tell you what, we both hung up lighter and freer.

That's because God uses prayer to bring a lighter load, and He uses others to carry it with us.

In one of our reflection questions, you identified negative words and soundtracks that play in your mind. **Who could you call to share those old thoughts with and to ask for prayer? When do you plan to do this today?**

> God uses prayer to bring a lighter load, and He uses others to carry it with us.

Be courageous, friend. God wants us to be healthy and to be whole, and community plays a part in that. So, take the step of asking a friend to pray with you and for you today.

WHAT OTHER PEOPLE THINK

I spend time with a sweet young high school girl every now and then. I've known her family since before she was born, and now that she's grown up, we carve out intentional time to hang out and talk about life, faith, school, boys, cross-country—all of it. The mentoring is so sweet; she teaches me so much too!

Recently, this young girl had a chance to lead the Wednesday morning Bible study on Psalm 23 for the Fellowship of Christian Athletes at her school. After getting together with me to talk about it, she felt excited and ready. In presenting her teaching that morning, she also practiced being vulnerable about her parents' divorce and discussing how this psalm has been an anchor for her. She later sent me a text that said, "It's hard to share God's Word when I care so much about what other people think. It's really annoying. How do you get through that?"

I couldn't have said it any better. Having an approval addiction is really annoying. I know because I have fallen into the people-pleasing pit one too many times myself. Down in that pit there is no sustenance, no water, nothing nourishing.

What pits do you fall into most? Achievement? The admiration of others? Success? Perfectionism? Consumerism?

How would you answer that text from my sweet young friend? How do you get through caring what other people think?

Here's what I texted back:

It is SO annoying. I continually have to climb out of the people-pleasing pit. I can sidestep it if I practice a few thoughts. 1. I need to say what God wants me to say, not what others want me to say. 2. This may result in disappointing people and that's okay. 3. I want to please God, not others. This is a process, friend! In it with you.

Later, I sent her to Galatians 1:10, as I love the way it speaks so well to this starvation for approval from others.

Look up Galatians 1:10 (NLT) and write out the verse in the space below.

According to this verse, who do we serve?

Why is pleasing people not our goal?

God is the One who made us, and He knows exactly who we are. Our fellow humans around us? They didn't knit us in our mother's womb, they don't know the number of hairs on our heads. They have been created too. When I put God in His proper place in my life—on the throne—then I can see more clearly that He is the One I serve, not the opinions of others. The voices quiet around me, and I can listen for just His. He made me. He sees me. He delights in me. He accepts me. I have nothing to fear and nothing to prove. I have the joy of living life with Him. I don't have to prove I am worthy of being His daughter. I already am.

In what areas do you feel like you have to prove something about yourself?

> As a people pleaser, your instinct to relieve the presence of any discomfort in yourself and others is driving your life. Therefore, you experience tremendous discomfort within relationships. You're motivated primarily by feelings of inadequacy and a consuming fear that you won't be accepted or approved of.
> **ILENE STRAUSS COHEN**

End today by taking a moment to close your eyes and imagine God's face shining upon you in pure delight. He accepts you just as you are, and He loves going with you on the errands He has given you to do. Imagine Him holding out His hand and saying, "Let's do today together. I want to be with you, not have you prove yourself to Me. I already wholeheartedly approve."

THE PRACTICE OF PRAYER

A helpful way for me to pray is to slowly write out one verse in a journal. Then, I write out any feelings, thoughts, frustrations, hopes, and prayers to God about the content of that verse. Often, writing slows down my brain and helps me clear what's inside my starving soul.

So today, that's what we're going to do. I'm leaving room here for you to practice journaling prayer below.

Slowly write out Romans 15:7 below. Let the reality that you are fully accepted, loved, and pleasing to God sink in.

Christ has accepted you, and therefore, you can accept yourself—all of yourself. The good, bad, ugly. You don't have to run around looking for validation. Your identity includes being accepted by Christ, and that's all you need. Think about this truth as you journal your prayers in response below. I've included some of my favorite journaling prompts if you need them.

Romans 15:7

God, I am . . .

God, You are . . .

God, I need . . .

God, thank You . . .

SING A NEW SONG

I am a sucker for *The Greatest Showman*. I love every single song in that movie. The first time I saw it, I laughed, and I cried, and I adored the whole thing. Now, the film's soundtrack is one my kids and I will often dance around to together, waving wooden spoons like ringmasters. It's just that good, you guys.

I once heard a friend say that she views the psalms like soundtracks. Sometimes you have to find the right psalm to match how you are feeling today, what you need, and what would play well with your life right now.

Often, I pair a song with a walk, and it becomes prayer. It's a time to listen to God—to hear Him singing over me. It's a chance to change the soundtrack in my mind and sing a new song in my heart.

One particular day, I was on a walk just before an upcoming speaking event. The narrative running through my mind wasn't helpful.

I can't teach.

I shouldn't be doing this.

I'm not qualified to preach.

I'm not sure God can use me here.

Realizing that narrative was starving me from my true identity, I knew it was time to change the soundtrack. It was time to let the truth get stuck on repeat instead.

So I turned on "The Blessing" by Kari Jobe. That song was such nourishment for my identity that day. These lyrics specifically became my new song:

May His favor be upon you
And a thousand generations
And your family and your children.

Do you have a song that speaks God's truth to you? Write the name of that song here. Then, write the lyrics that resonate with your heart along with it.

It's so important to change the soundtrack in our minds. To extinguish the fiery lies and sing a new song over who we are. Because that's exactly what our enemy is aiming at: our identity. In Scripture, Paul wants us to understand that we have a mighty power available to us when it comes to the lies the enemy may use to starve us.

Turn to Ephesians 6. Read verses 10-18. As you read, underline the pieces of armor we have. Feel free to list them below as well!

According to verse 16, what extinguishes the fiery arrows (the lies) of the evil one?

One of the best ways we can practice holding up that shield of faith is to sing a new song over our starving souls. I love these verses about God singing over us and us having a new song in our mouths. As you read, underline the words that stand out to you the most.

> He put a new song in my mouth,
>   a song of praise to our God.
> Many will see and fear,
>   and put their trust in the LORD.
>
> PSALM 40:3

The LORD your God is in your midst,
> a mighty one who will save;
he will rejoice over you with gladness;
> he will quiet you by his love;
he will exult over you with loud singing.

ZEPHANIAH 3:17

What kind of new song do you need to sing to God?

If you could have God sing anything over you, what would it be?

Friend, when the truth of who we are is threatened by the lies the enemy wants us to believe, let's commit to listening to the songs of our God. Let's commit to changing the soundtrack so we can sing a new song—a true song—about who we are in Him.

THE PRACTICE OF PRAYER

It's time to sing a new song, friend!

So today, find a song to listen to that speaks of who you are. Either take a moment to sit and listen, take a walk and listen, or play it in the car while you're on the go.

This doesn't have to be a big time investment, but it is a big soul investment. Let God's truth sing over you. Then, sing it back to Him as a prayer of truth and gratitude.

To help you get started, here's what is on my current playlist of songs that speak to my heart.

"Promises" by Maverick City Music

"The Blessing" by Kari Jobe

"Joy of the Lord" by Maverick City Music

"Firm Foundation (He Won't)" by Maverick City Music

"Graves into Gardens" by Elevation Worship

"You Say" by Lauren Daigle

"Rescue" by Lauren Daigle

"Hold On to Me" by Lauren Daigle

"Springtime" by Chris Renzema

"There Was Jesus" by Zach Williams and Dolly Parton

TEACH US HOW TO PRAY

Waking up to a full in-box, I started to read my emails. This always happens. On the days I get to teach a two-minute story on the YouVersion Bible App, I wake up to a ton of emails. While most of them are encouraging and kind, there's always the handful that . . . well, aren't. This day, one particular email was laced with critique about the way I presented myself on camera.

Even though thirty more emails came in glowing about my teaching, this was the one that chased me around all day. I had given this one email—one that probably took about three minutes for this person to write—about three hours of worry.

This seems way out of balance. Why do we give someone so much of our energy and time when they only gave us a minute or two? Shouldn't we be able to let it go and move on?

Easier said than done for most of us, right?

As we continue to think about enjoying our identity and leaving the opinions of others behind, it seems we need some good words from our Father to hold on to. This way, we aren't tossed here and there by every word said to us by others. Since we are thinking about the weight of words, Jesus' words hold mighty power and substantial truth—much more power and truth than a three-minute e-mail from a random person.

So far this week, we have explored praying with a friend, journaling, and worship music as ways to hear from God. There's a variety of ways to practice listening to God because He made us all different! Today, we're going to look specifically at one of the most common, and that's prayer.

Jesus gave us a touchstone when it comes to prayer—a model we can follow.

We know this now as the Lord's Prayer. As we read it together today, I want to consider some beautiful truths that God reveals to us in these words.

Before you turn to read this Scripture, ask God for fresh eyes to see and hear this section. Now, turn to Matthew 6:9-13. If you can, maybe read it in a translation you don't normally use for a new perspective. What words speak to you from this prayer?

Six themes emerge here in this prayer—six truths about who God is to us. I turn to these themes for nourishment when I'm starved to remember God's character and His promises.

Let's take some time to think through each promise in this prayer. Take your time thinking about each aspect of God's character that Jesus mentions. As we continue to thirst for our identity, we find so much of it in these words.

Write a prayer sentence or two under each theme. I've included a sentence with each to get you started.

Father: You are my good Father, and I have a good family.

Worship: I was created for worship, and Your holy name alone is worthy of my worship.

Heaven is here: God, your Kingdom way has invaded our hearts. May it continue to invade our world, our city, our neighborhood, and more.

Provision: God, I trust You to provide everything I need.

Forgiveness: God, Your forgiveness of me seems to be directly linked to my forgiveness of others. Help me to be a generous forgiver.

Rescue: God, I need Your strength and Your protection from our enemy.

Of the themes we went over here, circle the one you most need today.

Expand on your prayer over that theme here. Ask God to use it specifically to speak to what's on your heart.

When I feel lost for words, I come back to these themes. What does my heart need right now? What part of my identity feels shaken?

Do I need to know I have a Father who loves me?

Do I need to turn away from my self-worship and worship God?

Do I need to be more involved in helping Your Kingdom invade my neighborhood?

Do I need to remember that God will take care of me?

Do I need to confess my sin and find forgiveness? Or come to forgive another?

Do I need to know God's rescuing strength today?

Jesus has not left us without help or without hope. He has given us a way to pray, a way to come, a way to commune with Him so we can embrace our identity as His children.

THE PRACTICE OF PRAYER

Today, we spent good time in the Lord's Prayer. I am so grateful for humble learners who show us how to ask for what we need, just as the disciples did here!

Take that theme you circled above and use it as your prayer today. Ask God to remind you of it often.

For example, I chose the theme of rescue. So, I am asking God for that to be my theme today. Even if I just whisper the word "rescue" throughout the day, in the car, on a walk, in between job tasks, or as I go to bed, this will remind me of who God is and who I am because of Him.

TREASURES IN YOUR HEART

We know that God speaks in all kinds of ways. Today, we want to remember the ways He has used the family of God to speak to us. We want to look at how He nourishes our identity through the words of others.

How have the encouraging words of others given you confidence and hope?

Who has said something to you about how you are made, what gifts you have, or how treasured you are that gave you life? Write about that here.

When I think about this idea of speaking life over others, I think about Mary. She was holding the Son of God in her arms when shepherds ran to tell her an angel parade had just shown up in the sky. The shepherds came and worshiped her baby. And then Luke records something sweet and wonderful that Mary did in response.

Write down what Luke says Mary did in Luke 2:19.

This makes me think about the ancient, gorgeous oak tree down the lane from our old house. When my babies were little, we would watch squirrels hunt and gather around that tree, storing acorns away for winter. It seems Mary also may have been storing beauty for the arrival of winter.

Treasures to turn to when things weren't turning out as planned.

When the ground froze.

When darkness came.

When winter arrived.

When starvation loomed.

When her son was wrongly accused and unjustly killed.

Today, let's remember the treasures we can store up in our own hearts for when we need them.

What's a treasure you're remembering today about who you are? A word given to you from someone else? A truth that encouraged you? A kindness that resonated in your heart? Try to think of at least three encouragements spoken to or about you through the years. Write them down here.

Why were these words meaningful to you?

I have collected some treasures in my heart through the years. Recently I was introduced to a beloved church community before I spoke. I have come to love being a guest preacher in this place, and this day, the words the pastor shared as an introduction for me weren't just a nice welcome. They were words of direct encouragement to me and a confirmation of the calling on my life. I will never forget what he said. I came home and wrote it down. It spoke in direct contrast to the lies that have threatened to starve this calling and my identity in it. God knew I needed it to be nourished so I could keep going.

If nothing like this comes to mind for you right now, let me give a word of encouragement.

Let's take a slow moment with this verse. Who lives in you now?

> I have been crucified with Christ and I no longer live, but Christ lives in me. The life I now live in the body, I live by faith in the Son of God, who loved me and gave himself for me. **GALATIANS 2:20, NIV**

Fill in the blank here.

The life I now live in the body, I live by _____ in the Son of God."

Write down the last two verbs in this verse here.

If nothing else, treasure this truth in your heart:

The Son of God LOVED you and GAVE Himself for you.

You were worth Jesus giving His whole life for. You are so incredibly loved that Jesus said, "She is mine. And I would die for her."

And friend, He did.

When we're starving to remember who we are, where our value lies, and what we're called to in this life, we can start with Jesus. We can remember what He did for us because of who He is and who we are to Him.

There, we can find nourishment.

There, we can find real identity.

THE PRACTICE OF PRAYER

Richard Foster gives us the practice of releasing and receiving God's truth and peace through an exercise called Palms Down, Palms Up.[1]

Today, begin by closing your eyes. Open your palms, face down. Tell God everything that comes to mind that you want to release to Him. Maybe it's a negative narrative. Maybe it's anxious worries. Maybe it's last night's fight with your husband. Maybe it's uncontested sin. Whatever is weighing on you, tell God about it. Release it to Him.

When you have released all you can, turn your palms up. Tell God you are ready to receive whatever He has for you. You are listening. You are ready to receive peace, hope, love, joy, or anything He wants to give. You are ready to receive quiet, calm, or just the truth that you are loved according to the Scripture we read today.

Enjoy this practice that connects your mind, heart, and body. Let God speak truth to the core of who you are.

PEANUT BUTTER AND JELLY BARS

When I hear peanut butter and jelly bars, it takes me back to the sweetness and ease of childhood—to the carefree state of being a beloved child, adored by her good father. This recipe comes from one of my favorite food bloggers, Wholesomely Hannah. Her original recipe for Almond Cherry Bars calls for almond butter and fresh cherries. In this recipe, I did a slight twist and used all-natural peanut butter and fresh strawberries, but any fruit will do. I double this recipe to make a birthday cake for my oldest.

Filling

2 cups strawberries
1 tbsp. honey

¼ tsp. salt
½ tbsp. coconut flour

Crust/Crumb Topping

1½ cups almond flour
⅓ cup coconut flour
1 tsp. baking soda
2 tsp. cinnamon
¼ tsp. salt
½ cup pecans, chopped

½ cup butter, melted
¼ cup honey
2 tbsp. no-sugar, all-natural
   peanut butter
2 tsp. vanilla
1 tsp. apple cider vinegar

Instructions

1. Preheat the oven to 350°F. Lightly grease a 9 × 9 baking pan with cooking spray.

2. To make the strawberry filling, combine strawberries, honey, and salt in a stovetop pan. Cook over medium heat for 10 minutes.

3. Stir in coconut flour and remove from heat. Mash berries with a fork and set aside.

4. To make the crust, in a large mixing bowl combine almond flour, coconut flour, baking soda, cinnamon, salt, and chopped pecans. Stir well.

5. Add melted butter, honey, peanut butter, vanilla, and apple cider vinegar to flour mixture. Beat with an electric mixer until a crumbly dough forms.

6. Press ⅔ of the dough into the pan and bake for 8 minutes.

7. Pour strawberry filling over baked crust and spread to cover fully.

8. Sprinkle the leftover dough mixture over the filling, distributing evenly.

9. Bake for 20 minutes, or until the crumb topping is golden brown.

10. Let the dessert cool completely before slicing into squares.

11. Refrigerate and see how long it lasts!

Adapted with permission from wholesomelyhannah.net /scd-cherry-pecan-crumb-bars.

STARVED FOR PEACE

Questions for Discussion

THE PROBLEM
What is starving us in our longing for peace?

THE PROMISE
What Scriptures have been feeding your soul lately?

THE PRACTICE
What spiritual practice can satiate you when your soul is starved for peace?

PERSONAL REFLECTION
Choose a question and take a moment to journal.

- What atmosphere do you create around you when you worship control?
- When you think about practically seeking God's kingdom first, what does that look like?
- Copy this verse, slowly, in your own handwriting: "Seek first his kingdom and his righteousness, and all these things will be given to you as well. Therefore do not worry about tomorrow, for tomorrow will worry about itself. Each day has enough trouble of its own" (Matthew 6:33-34). What speaks to you in this passage?

STARVED FOR PEACE

To get the most out of this week's study, read chapter 7 of *Starved*.

WAVES OF ANXIETY, ANCHORS OF PEACE

"Taking your worries to God doesn't mean it will all stop being hard. But it does mean there can be peace."

These thoughts echoed in my ears as I left the podcast studio that day. I had interviewed my dear friend and Bible study author Barb Roose as a guest on the *Three Words* podcast, where I occasionally moonlight as the host. The three words she shared that day: "Worrying solves nothing."[1]

Isn't that the truth, friend?

Our twelve-minute chat was filled with wisdom and ideas related to those three words, but her final statement on peace is what I carried with me. I love that she didn't try to guarantee a pass from suffering. Sadly, we all know that isn't the reality of living in this fallen world. She did, however, tell us peace was possible in the middle of the tumultuous waves of anxiety. That is a promise I want to hold on to. Maybe it's one you want to hold on to as well.

Because friend, if there's one thing I know is true for most of us, it's that anxiety has starved us of so much. The most significant? The deep, lasting peace that will nourish us.

Have you ever noticed that early in the morning and late at night are ripest for things like worry and anxiety? Medical studies back this up.[2] And I feel it, friend. So often before my feet hit the ground in the morning, my brain hits me with ALL the tasks, how behind I am, and every puzzle that needs the missing pieces for my day, my family, or my work. With that, before I changed my phone pattern, I used to reach for my phone and start reading emails right away. Talk about a stressful wake-up routine!

I have changed a lot of my morning routine to eliminate worry and to embrace peace. I don't check email or social media until later in the morning. And before I go downstairs to get coffee and my Bible, I go to my knees and claim God as King of my heart, my day, my tasks, my family—an act of submitting my worries and anxieties to Him.

A way of anchoring myself to the Giver of peace.

And friend, that's what I believe we actually need. When we're starving for peace, we can find it by anchoring our thoughts, our hearts, our worries, our anxieties to the One who gives it in real, lasting ways.

So, when waves of anxiety hit, how do we stay anchored in peace? There are many ways to keep anxiety at bay and live in peace. There's therapy (a personal favorite), exercise, meditation, breathing exercises, medicine, prayer, among others. But first and foremost, there is God's Word.

Don't worry, I'm not going to tell you that simply reading your Bible will make it all go away. That's not helpful or nourishing. But I will tell you that knowing God's Word helps bring peace. It's the best place we can start. It's the best place we can return to time and again. It's where we can find our anchor.

As we close this study, my prayer is that we'll walk this final week together toward the peace that only God can give. Yes, we're almost done with this study, but we're just beginning our journey out of starvation and into spiritual nourishment. We're just starting the daily road of laying down what isn't feeding us and picking up what will.

This week, that's God's Word.

So, one last time, let's dive deep together.

Let's trust God to help us find the anchor of peace in our waves of anxiety.

THE LINK BETWEEN ANXIETY AND GRATITUDE

Take a moment to pray, asking God to speak to you through His Word today.

Then, read the Scripture below. Underline any place you see the word *peace* and the things we are called to do in order to experience peace.

> Do not be anxious about anything, but in every situation, by prayer and petition, with thanksgiving, present your requests to God. And the peace of God, which transcends all understanding, will guard your hearts and your minds in Christ Jesus.
>
> Finally, brothers and sisters, whatever is true, whatever is noble, whatever is right, whatever is pure, whatever is lovely, whatever is admirable—if anything is excellent or praiseworthy—think about such things. Whatever you have learned or received or heard from me, or seen in me—put it into practice. And the God of peace will be with you.
>
> **PHILIPPIANS 4:6-9, NIV**

Let's slowly unpack this one together.

Did Paul tell us not to be anxious for most things? Some things? A few things?

Instead of being anxious, what does Paul tell us to do?

> Practicing gratitude while talking to God is part of the way we can experience peace.

I love this passage for a number of reasons, but one is that Paul gives us a little formula to follow here:

prayer + thanksgiving = peace that passes all understanding

I love that Paul goes out of his way to make sure we know it's more than just prayer. Practicing gratitude while talking to God is part of the way we can experience peace. The power of gratitude can take your mind off your anxious thoughts and center it on all the grace you see around you. It's a helpful practice to usher in peace.

One of my favorite ways to do what Paul recommends is with some journaling prompts.

Today, let's take our time and journal out these thoughts.

What am I anxious about? Name everything that comes to mind.

What can I do to remedy this anxiety? For example, make a phone call, rearrange my schedule, do the top three items on my to-do list.

What is there that I cannot do but God can? Write out a specific prayer request about what you cannot change about your worries. For instance, I can't change hearts or I can't be in two places at once. Be sure to include some thanksgiving in there, just as Paul suggests.

What am I grateful for? List at least five things to be grateful for. Start small. There can be gratitude in all things, big and small.

THE PRACTICE OF PEACE

Today, let's end our time with one minute of meditating on a truth found in Scripture. We can do this by focusing our breath and attention on that truth.

Repeat this truth slowly for one minute as you breathe in and out.

Inhale: I give You my anxiety.
Exhale: I welcome Your peace.

WHAT WE THINK ABOUT

Are there days you wish you could change your brain? Do you wish you could just take out the anxious thoughts and replace them with peaceful and calming thoughts instead?

Good news, friend: this may be more possible than you think!

The beautiful work of Dr. Caroline Leaf has helped me see that the brain has neuroplasticity—the ability to change.[1] This is important because our thoughts lead to feelings, and those feelings cause us to act. If we want to act out of peace, we've got to think about peace first!

What's one thing you tend to think about often that doesn't give you peace?

Notice how, in yesterday's passage, Paul gave us eight clear prompts to think about when it comes to anxiety. Instead of focusing on the worries, fears, anxieties, or circumstances surrounding us, we can think on these things instead.

Read the passage below once again.

Do not be anxious about anything, but in every situation, by prayer and petition, with thanksgiving, present your requests to God. And the peace of God, which transcends all understanding, will guard your hearts and your minds in Christ Jesus.

Finally, brothers and sisters, whatever is true, whatever is noble, whatever is right, whatever is pure, whatever is lovely, whatever is admirable—if anything is excellent or praiseworthy—think about such things. Whatever you have learned or received or heard from me, or seen in me—put it into practice. And the God of peace will be with you.

PHILIPPIANS 4:6-9, NIV

Paul tells us specifically to think on some things. Write down the things that Paul tells us to think about or focus on in the passage.

When we're starved for peace (or even when we're not), we are called to put into practice thinking on the things of God. Why? Because that's where our minds find rest, nourishment, satisfaction. That's where we find peace.

So for today, we are going to use the practice of writing to think about these things.

Take your time, slowly writing a sentence to describe what each word below could look like in your life. Let your mind meditate on each truth, praying for God's help to see what it might mean to find peace in thinking about each of these things.

True (real)

Noble (honorable)

Right (morally good)

Pure (not mixed or adulterated)

Lovely (beautiful)

Admirable (deserving respect)

Excellent (outstanding)

Praiseworthy (commendable)

Of the words listed above, which one will you focus on this week? Write a prayer to close today, asking God to help shift your thoughts to that word— the thing that will give you peace.

THE PRACTICE OF PEACE

Notice what Paul says will happen when we think on these things: "And the God of peace will be with you." God is the God of peace. That means that not only is peace available, but the GOD of peace will be with you. He owns peace. It is His to give.

Today, let's end our time with one minute of meditating on a truth found in Scripture. We can do this by focusing our breath and attention on this truth from God's Word.

Repeat this slowly for one minute as you breathe in and out.

Inhale: God, You are lovely.
Exhale: You are the God of peace.

WHERE IS YOUR TREASURE?

So often, anxiety is about the future. It focuses on all the "What ifs?" in life.

What if when my daughter gets on the bus she is bullied?

What if someone I love is tragically taken away?

What if I lose my job and can't pay my bills?

What if?

It's the question that starves our minds of peace. And usually, it's a question we ask about the things that we hold dear—the things that we treasure.

My pastor (also a licensed counselor) says that Jesus instructs us to take our treasures and put them into Heaven's hands. Let God hold onto them for the day while you go about the work He has for you. This way, our attention isn't divided.

Easier said than done, friend! Our attention is so easily divided when we're anxious. We are physically in one place, but mentally we are somewhere else. Mentally, we're playing out the "What ifs?"

This is the exact meaning of anxiety. The Greek word for anxiety is *merimnaō*, which means to tear apart or to divide. This is what anxiety does to us. It divides us between the present and the future. And in that place, we aren't free to live our life fully.

So how do we live wholeheartedly at peace in one place? Like anything else, we practice. Just as my pastor suggested, we practice giving our treasures to God.

Read Matthew 6:19-21. Where does Jesus tell us to store our treasure?

Do not store up for yourselves treasures on earth, where moths and vermin destroy, and where thieves break in and steal. But store up for yourselves treasures in heaven, where moths and vermin do not destroy, and where thieves do not break in and steal. For where your treasure is, there your heart will be also.

MATTHEW 6:19-21, NIV

Does Jesus tell us not to have treasures?

What does He say about our treasure and our hearts?

So, how do we actually do this? What does this look like?

I have found this little process I've called Treasure Storing to be helpful.

To start, let's answer the questions below. I've included some examples to help you think about your own responses.

What is it that I am anxious about? (My child being safe.)

What am I treasuring in this anxiety? What am I protecting? Be as honest as possible. (I am treasuring my precious child.)

Does this treasure align with God's Kingdom? (Yes, God definitely treasures my daughter. He made her and loves her.)

How can I give my treasure to God? He can either keep it safe in heaven, or He can help me let it go. (God, I open my hands as a symbol of giving You my child. I trust that You will do what is best with my child, my treasure. Keep her for me so I am freed up to do what You have for me today.)

I open my hands and practice handing my treasure to God in heaven. I imagine Him taking care of my treasure for the day. And if my treasure doesn't align with God's Kingdom and His purposes, then I practice opening my hands and letting go of that treasure. So, I am either handing my treasure to God to hold, or I'm letting go of the treasure altogether. Both require open hands.

Sometimes I practice this several times a day! Giving, and giving, and giving my treasure to God to store for me. Laying down, and down, and down my pride, my selfishness, my envy, my comparison. This helps me to be wholehearted and openhanded in the tasks in front of me.

It helps me find the nourishment of peace my anxious mind is starved for.

What I find so beautiful is that right after Jesus teaches about storing our treasures and our hearts, He talks about worry. I think that's because they are so very deeply connected.

Read Matthew 6:25-34. Write out verse 26 below.

Verse 26 speaks to us about our worry and our value. How does this verse bring you comfort?

Close today by resting in the truth of Jesus' words. Let your mind find peace in turning over your worries and handing Him your treasures. Write a prayer here, asking for His peace to turn over your treasures to the Lord's hands.

THE PRACTICE OF PEACE

Today, let's end our time with one minute of meditating on a truth found in Scripture. We can do this by focusing our breath and attention on this truth from God's Word.

Repeat this slowly for one minute as you breathe in and out.

Inhale: God, I give You my treasures.
Exhale: I let go of treasures that are not heavenly.

WHAT IF?

Yesterday, we talked about the questions of "What if?" that threaten to cut us off from the nourishing peace God offers us each day. Today, we're going to dive deeper into what we can do with those questions.

Sometimes I am anxious about decisions I have to make or ones I have already made. Does this happen to you? I start to worry about how it will all turn out or whether I made the wrong decision. Anxiety knows no bounds!

Is there a choice you have made or need to make that is causing you anxiety? What is it?

Write three "What ifs?" on your mind about that choice:

What if _____

What if _____

What if _____

What if I told you the solution to "What if?" is one simple truth?
God will take care of me.

Let's see if this truth really holds up. Let's see what happens if we take our anxieties to the worst-case scenario. If we sink the ship, will God still be there at the bottom of it all? Will God really take care of us in our choices? Let's ask some questions to find out.

Question: What if I make this choice and I regret it?

Answer: God will take care of me. After all, He took care of Peter after he denied Jesus three times. Talk about regret . . . and restoration.

Question: What if I make this decision and it's a terrible mistake?

Answer: God will take care of me. After all, He took care of David in his choices, the good and the bad. Surely God will take care of me in this choice.

Question: What if this choice turns out to be the hardest path I have ever walked?

Answer: God will take care of me. After all, He took care of His own Son after He faced betrayal, persecution, beatings, crucifixion, and death. He brought a resurrection.

In any possible scenario, we can bank on God taking care of us.

No choice is risk-free.

No choice comes with all the guarantees.

But in every choice, you can trust the Maker as your safety net.

Does that mean this choice is free from struggle? Or that God will make an easy way? Or that you are now free from more stress, emotion, and fatigue to come?

Don't I wish the answer was yes. But it's not.

However, it does mean God will be with you in this decision. He will provide peace. He will not abandon you. He will not forsake you. He is for you. He adores you. He delights in You.

You can trust your good, good Father as you make a choice in the middle of a not-so-good situation.

Read Genesis 50:20-21. As you read, jot down some thoughts about the way Joseph speaks to his brothers.

> You can trust your good, good Father as you make a choice in the middle of a not-so-good situation.

Joseph is a huge encouragement to me when it comes to finding peace in my "What if?" questions. His brothers hated how much his father adored him, and they sold him to Egyptian slaves. He was in jail for years until God did something miraculous and put him as second in command of all of Egypt. What redemption! And then the same brothers who betrayed him came begging for food and aid. And Joseph? He forgave them. He provided for the brothers who had turned him over to be forgotten and forsaken! God had not forgotten or forsaken Joseph in all of this.

In his worst-case scenario, God was there.

I am encouraged on two levels. First, his brothers made a HUGE and terrible mistake. They were wicked and sold him into slavery. This was an evil choice. And God still worked it together for their good! How incredibly compassionate and gracious.

And second, Joseph was wronged. In so many ways in the course of his life, beginning with being sold by his brothers. He experienced injustice after injustice. And God still worked it together for their good!

God is compassionate and gracious, slow to anger, and abounding in lovingkindness and faithfulness, am I right?

Doesn't this remind you of another passage saying this same thing? **Look up Romans 8:28 (NIV) and fill in the blanks below.**

We know that _____ God works _____
of those who love him, who _____ according to his purpose.

All things are NOT good, but God works all things FOR our good. I am sure Paul was thinking of Joseph's story when he penned these words.

Write "God will take care of me" in big letters across your three "What Ifs?" we started with on page 178. This is the truth.

THE PRACTICE OF PEACE

We feed our anxious minds with the nourishment of peace found in God's Word. To help you do that today, meditate on these passages:

My God will supply every need of yours according to his riches in glory in Christ Jesus.
PHILIPPIANS 4:19

Behold, God is my helper;
 the Lord is the upholder of my life.
PSALM 54:4

Casting all your anxieties on him, because he cares for you.
1 PETER 5:7

Today, let's end our time with one minute of meditating on a truth found in Scripture. We can do this by focusing our breath and attention on this truth from God's Word.

Repeat this slowly for one minute as you breathe in and out.

Inhale: God will take care of me.
Exhale: God is working for my good.

THE UNSHAKABLE KINGDOM OF GOD

You've made it, friend. The last day of the last week of our six-week journey. I know you have found nourishment on these pages—because God has given us good things to eat here. I am so proud of you!

As we close out our week on finding anchors of peace in our waves of anxiety, I find great comfort in words from theologian and author James Bryan Smith. Regarding anxiety and the truth of who we are, Smith writes, "I am a child of God, one in whom Christ dwells, and I am living in the unshakable kingdom of God."[1]

The unshakable Kingdom of God.

It's such a beautiful, comforting phrase. And friend, we have been shaken. We have been through so much in our lifetimes but specifically in the most recent years.

A pandemic.

Wars.

Grief.

Pain.

Political and racial unrest.

Deep loss.

And yet, God is still on the throne and His Kingdom will not be shaken. Even if we are, He remains steady. I often turn to Psalm 46 when it feels like everything is shaken, as if mountains are being thrown into the heart of the sea—even if it's my own mountain of worry thrown into the sea of my heart.

Read Psalm 46:1-5.

According to the last verse, why can't the city be destroyed?

> God is our refuge and strength,
>   always ready to help in times of trouble.
> So we will not fear when earthquakes come
>   and the mountains crumble into the sea.
> Let the oceans roar and foam.
>   Let the mountains tremble as the waters surge! . . .
>
> A river brings joy to the city of our God,
>   the sacred home of the Most High.
> God dwells in that city; it cannot be destroyed.
>   From the very break of day, God will protect it.
> **PSALM 46:1-5, NLT**

Friend, what a gift these words are to us! When everything around us feels shaken, we can stand confidently knowing we won't be destroyed. God dwells in us, and because of that, we cannot be broken, destroyed, or beaten down by the waves of anxiety.

Another psalm I love when it comes to peace is Psalm 16. Turn to it and read the entire psalm slowly. Write down verses 8-9 in the space below. Let the truth in this passage sink in. Feel the peace, the unshakable truth, the security that comes from God's Word.

This reminds me of when Peter took that crazy step of faith and walked on water toward Jesus. But something happens when he shifts his focus.

Read Matthew 14:22-32. Who did Peter cry out to for help in verse 30?

Peter's choice to look to the Lord calls Psalm 16 to mind. He is the only One we can turn to. When we're starving, when we're scared, when we're anxious—we can put our eyes on the Lord for help. Because, friend, when we keep our eyes on the Lord, we will not be shaken.

I know because I've experienced it myself. I'm sure you have too! Like Peter, I've had to put my eyes on the Lord when anxiety has threatened to take me down under the waves. I've had to trust in the unshakable Kingdom of God when life has left me shaken. And I know there is truth here because there are so many promises like this in the Bible.

Read a few of my favorites inspired by Scripture, circling the words that stand out to you as you do. You can even write the Scripture below each one to remind you where this truth comes from.

When we keep the truth of the eternal Kingdom of God in focus, we will not be shaken. (See Luke 1:33.)

When we remember that the moment after we die, we will be in glory, we will not be shaken. (See Luke 23:43; Philippians 1:21.)

When we set our eyes on the good promises of God, we know that He who promises is faithful. (See Hebrews 10:23.)

Take your time to look back at the pages of this week's study. What stands out to you when it comes to reclaiming your peace in waves of anxiety?

What's one step you will take this week to find satisfaction in peace when anxiety threatens to starve you?

THE PRACTICE OF PEACE

Today, let's end our time with one minute of meditating on a truth found in Scripture. We can do this by focusing our breath and attention on this truth from God's Word.

Repeat this slowly for one minute as you breathe in and out.

Inhale: I am a child of God.
Exhale: I live in the unshakable Kingdom of God.

THE SEIFFERT FATHEAD DOUGH

I kept seeing keto fathead dough recipes zipping around the Internet. But since my son can't do any soft cheeses (only cheese aged over 30 days), we couldn't make it with mozzarella. Cue the provolone! You can use this dough like we do to make a yummy bread to dip into marinara sauce. Or make it into a pizza and top it with marinara, pepperoni, and more cheese. Or add spinach, chicken, bacon, and ranch—the combinations are endless. And dare I say you'll make peace with that pizza craving?

Ingredients

16 slices provolone
2 eggs
⅓ cup coconut flour
¾ tsp. baking soda

¼ tsp. garlic powder
⅛ tsp. salt
olive oil (for greasing skillet and
    drizzling on top of dough)

Instructions

1. Preheat oven to 375°F.
2. Melt cheese in a big bowl in the microwave (melt for 1 minute at a time and mix, then repeat until fully melted).
3. While microwaving, grease an iron skillet with olive oil on the bottom and sides.
4. Add eggs, coconut flour, baking soda, garlic powder, and salt to the melted cheese and mix. (Sometimes I do this by hand because it's easier.) Flatten the dough inside the greased skillet.
5. Drizzle a little bit of olive oil onto the flattened dough.
6. Bake at 375°F for 10–12 minutes until golden brown. You could also broil for about 1 minute to make the dough crispy on top but still soft inside.

A FINAL WORD

DEAR FRIEND,

I have been praying for you on this journey. Praying for greater understanding, praying for heart change, and praying for lasting nourishment. I've been praying for you to experience Christ in a way that you haven't yet in your life. My hope is that in these pages, you have found Him to be a safe place—a nourishing Shepherd to satisfy your starving soul.

I am proud of you. You have shared your heart. You have tried new practices. You have encountered the Scriptures. You have made a change in your rhythms simply by picking up this study and walking through each day.

I am still in this with you. As this study comes to a close, I want to tell you that you are not alone in this journey. Keep coming to Jesus. Keep eating His good nourishment. Keep living. Keep slowing down. Keep Sabbathing. Keep pressing into the sacred silence. Keep taking the time to nourish your soul.

Because, if you don't have your soul, what do you have? As Jesus said it: "What do you benefit if you gain the whole world but lose your own soul? Is anything worth more than your soul?" (Matthew 16:26, NLT).

May you keep choosing paths of nourishment for your soul. May you eagerly pull up a seat at the King's banquet table full of peace, joy, justice, mercy, compassion, and grace.

I'll be right there with you when you do.

Amy

NOTES

SESSION 1: STARVED FOR CONNECTION

1. Trevor Wheelwright, "2022 Cell Phone Usage Statistics: How Obsessed Are We?" Reviews.org, January 24, 2022, https://www.reviews.org/mobile/cell-phone-addiction/.

SESSION 1, DAY 1: PUT DOWN THE PHONE, FRIEND

1. "What Is Compassion?" Greater Good Magazine, Greater Good Science Center at the University of California, Berkeley, accessed March 27, 2022, https://greatergood.berkeley.edu/topic/compassion/definition.
2. Aundi Kolber, *Try Softer: A Fresh Approach to Move Us out of Anxiety, Stress, and Survival Mode—and into a Life of Connection and Joy* (Carol Stream, IL: Tyndale, 2020), 118.

SESSION 1, DAY 4: THE GREAT MINT TAKEOVER

1. *Merriam-Webster*, s.v. "abounding (*adj.*)," accessed April 30, 2022, https://www.merriam-webster.com/dictionary/abounding.
2. "What Does It Mean That Christians Are Adopted by God?" Got Questions, accessed March 27, 2022, https://www.gotquestions.org/Christian-adoption.html.

SESSION 2, DAY 1: WHERE CYPRESS TREES GROW

1. Antonio Cruz, "The Cypress Trees Believe in God," trans. Roger Marshall, Evangelical Focus Europe, June 16, 2019, https://evangelicalfocus.com/magazine/4513/The-cypress-trees-believe-in-God.

SESSION 2, DAY 3: BELOVED? REALLY?

1. Ron Edmondson, "BELOVED, One of the Best Words in the Bible," *Ron Edmondson* (blog), December 27, 2009, https://ronedmondson.com/2009/12/beloved-one-of-the-best-words-in-the-bible.html.
2. "The Achiever: Enneagram Type Three," The Enneagram Institute, accessed March 27, 2022, https://www.enneagraminstitute.com/type-3. Also see Don Richard Riso and Russ Hudson, *The Wisdom of the Enneagram: The Complete Guide to Psychological and Spiritual Growth for the Nine Personality Types* (New York, NY: Bantam, 1999), 153–155.
3. "Achiever: Enneagram Type Three."

SESSION 2, DAY 5: UNMASKING THE WORLD FOR WHAT IT IS

1. Henri J. M. Nouwen, *Life of the Beloved: Spiritual Living in a Secular World* (New York: Crossroad, 2002), 59.

SESSION 3: STARVED FOR SABBATH
1. Marva J. Dawn, *Keeping the Sabbath Wholly: Ceasing, Resting, Embracing, Feasting* (Grand Rapids, MI: Eerdmans, 1989), 15–16.

SESSION 3, DAY 2: STOP TRYING AND START TRUSTING
1. Dawn, *Keeping the Sabbath Wholly*.

SESSION 3, DAY 3: A FULL PLATE OF PEACE
1. Dawn, *Keeping the Sabbath Wholly*, 58–59.

SESSION 3, DAY 5: TIME TO FEAST
1. See Luke 22:19-20, Matthew 26:26-28, Mark 14: 22-24, 1 Corinthians 11:23-25.
2. Eugene H. Peterson, "The Pastor's Sabbath," *Christianity Today*, May 19, 2004, https://www.christianitytoday.com/pastors/leadership-books/prayerpersonalgrowth/lclead04-2.html.

SESSION 4, DAY 2: ACT JUSTLY
1. Adam Taylor, "What Does Social Justice Really Mean?" World Vision blog, February 20, 2012, https://www.worldvision.org/blog/social-justice-really-mean.

SESSION 4, DAY 3: LOVE MERCY
1. The Open Table, https://www.theopentable.org/.

SESSION 4, DAY 4: WALK HUMBLY
1. Rick Warren, *The Purpose Driven Life: What on Earth Am I Here For?* (Grand Rapids, MI: Zondervan, 2013), 262.
2. *Merriam-Webster*, s.v. "humility (*n.*)," accessed March 27, 2022, https://www.merriam-webster.com/dictionary/humility.

SESSION 4, DAY 5: IMAGO DEI
1. Tim Keller, *Justice and Generosity* (New York: Penguin, 2010), 2–3.
2. Latasha Morrison, *Be the Bridge: Pursuing God's Heart for Racial Reconciliation* (Colorado Springs, CO: Waterbrook, 2019), 121–122.

SESSION 5, DAY 5: TREASURE IN YOUR HEART
1. Richard J. Foster, *Celebration of Discipline: The Path to Spiritual Growth* (San Francisco: Harper, 1998), 30–31.

SESSION 6: STARVED FOR PEACE
1. Barb Roose, "Worrying Solves Nothing," December 6, 2021, interview by Amy Seiffert, Three Words podcast, episode 110, https://anchor.fm/threewords/episodes/110--Worrying-Solves-Nothing-w-Barb-Roose-e1b2gtn.
2. Leah Campbell, "Why Is My Anxiety Worse at Night?" Healthline, updated March 27, 2020, https://www.healthline.com/health/anxiety/anxiety-worse-at-night; Eleesha Lockett, "How to Ease Anxiety at Night," Healthline, December 20, 2018, https://www.healthline.com/health/anxiety/anxiety-at-night.

SESSION 6, DAY 2: WHAT WE THINK ABOUT

1. Caroline Leaf, "You Are Not a Victim of Your Biology," Dr. Leaf blog, October 3, 2018, https://drleaf.com/blogs/news/you-are-not-a-victim-of-your-biology.

SESSION 6, DAY 5: THE UNSHAKABLE KINGDOM OF GOD

1. James Bryan Smith, *The Good and Beautiful Life: Putting On the Character of Christ* (Downers Grove, IL: InterVarsity, 2009), 181.

ABOUT THE AUTHOR

AMY SEIFFERT is the author of *Grace Looks Amazing on You* and is on the teaching team at Brookside Church. She is an affiliate Cru staff member and a regular YouVersion Bible teacher. She loves to travel and speak (and try new foods on all her adventures!). Amy is married to her college sweetheart, Rob, and they live in Bowling Green, Ohio, with their three kids.

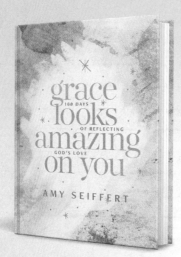
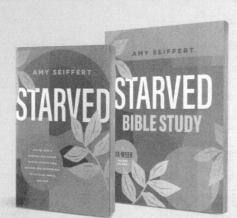